SH
One Man's Journeys to the High Country

Paul C. Carter

©Copyright 2011 by Paul C. Carter, Second Edition 2013

ISBN-13: 978-1466403666
ISBN-10: 1466403667

All rights reserved. No part of this book may be reproduced by any mechanical, photographic, or electronic process, or in the form of a phonographic recording, nor may be it stored in a retrieval system, transmitted, or otherwise be copied for public or private use—other than for "fair use" as brief quotations embodied in articles and reviews without prior written permission.

Printed by CreateSpace, a DBA of On-Demand Publishing LLC

Cover photograph by Steve Johnson

DEDICATION

*To the professional sheep guide—
whose expertise and passion for the sport makes it possible for
people like me to navigate the mountains safely and successfully*

Table of Contents

Preface	7
Introduction	9
Dall Sheep—1989	13
Stone Sheep—1990	29
Dall Sheep—1991	41
Rocky Mountain Bighorn Sheep—1992	55
Dall Sheep—1993	65
Stone Sheep—1994	77
Rocky Mountain Bighorn Sheep—1995	95
Dall Sheep—1996	109
Dall Sheep—1998	123
Desert Bighorn Sheep—1999	135
Rocky Mountain Bighorn Sheep—2003	149
Marco Polo Sheep—2004	163
Rocky Mountain Bighorn Sheep—2005	177
Desert Bighorn Sheep—2005	193
Dall Sheep—2007	203
Rocky Mountain Bighorn Sheep—2008	217
Desert Bighorn Sheep—2009	229
Fannin Sheep—2009	241
Stone Sheep—2010	253
Epilogue	265
Prologue to the Second Edition	267
Stone Sheep—2012	269

Preface

If you were to ask a hundred hunters, all of whom had experienced the full range of hunting opportunities that planet Earth has to offer, which type of hunting they deemed to be the most challenging, the nearly unanimous response would be mountain game—the world's sheep and goat species. Wherever they're found—the Rockies, Himalayas, the Southern Alps of New Zealand, the Caucasus or elsewhere—wild sheep and goats stir the imagination and try the souls of those who dare to meet them in their inhospitable domains.

The challenges are many: logistical, financial, physical, mental and emotional. Many hunting destinations, even within North America, require more than one full day of travel by car, commercial airplane, charter aircraft, boats and/or horses before a hunt even begins. Hunting mountain game is expensive, especially the sheep species. Some sheep hunts fetch outfitting or governmental fees which are among the highest in the world. It's a fact that climbing steep terrain is normally far more difficult than walking the same distance over level ground. Throw in the effects of altitude, weight on your back, boulder fields and all the other obstacles to balance and good footing that a mountain can throw at you, and navigation becomes even more exhausting. Bad weather, aching muscles, swarming insects, blistered feet, less-than-ideal nutrition and sleep deprivation conspire to degrade a hunter's sense of purpose and determination. The fittest person in the world will throw in the towel if his or her mental state has been degraded beyond a certain level by hardships such as multiple days stuck in a tent and constant frustration.

The bleakness conveyed in the previous paragraph is certainly offset by time amongst the most magnificent scenery our planet has to offer. Experiencing something truly wild—where raw nature rules and human beings are as inconsequential as a grain of sand at a beach—is very special. However, it's the sense of joy and accomplishment that accompanies a successful hunt for mountain game that exalts the experience and exhilarates the participant. All the trials, tribulations, aches and pains recede to insignificance as you kneel beside a hard-earned sheep or goat you've taken by means of fair chase in that animal's unforgiving domain.

The true essence of mountain hunting, not to mention its appeal, is found in this dichotomy of agony and ecstasy. Mountain hunting epitomizes the concept that something's true worth is best measured by the effort and sacrifices that are expended in its attainment. While it's just not possible for everyone to participate in the ups and downs or the despairs and glories the mountains offer, I hope this book fulfills the following goals: present a realistic look at what's involved in pursuing game in mountain settings while providing entertainment; and encourage those who are able to partake in this difficult but rewarding sport to do so.

INTRODUCTION

Thirty years ago I was barely aware that wild sheep existed. Although I was an enthusiastic whitetail deer hunter, the prospect of hunting other big-game species, let alone sheep, seemed decidedly distant. But in the mid-1980s something happened which would ultimately change my life in ways I couldn't possibly have foreseen. A wildlife cinematographer named George Klucky was appearing at a local high school auditorium to show footage of several big-game hunts conducted in the Wrangell Mountains of Alaska. Just for something to do, I decided to go, plop down the five-dollar admission fee and see what Alaska had to offer in the way of hunting opportunities.

Assuming a very prominent role in Mr. Klucky's personally narrated film was the all-white and majestic Dall sheep. The males of the species, otherwise known as rams, sported heavy-based amber horns that swept backwards from the skull in a continuous arc until the tips of the horns completed a full circle when viewed from the side. Viewed from the front, the horns flared towards the side as they reached their end-points. Equally impressive were the mountains these sheep called home. Tall, steep and devoid of trees, the vistas offered were stunning! In addition, the mountain environment seemed to project equal parts of challenge and danger, both of which were completely foreign to a northeastern deer hunter.

For me, the combined allure of the mountains and the sheep grabbed me in a way that I hadn't anticipated. With very little knowledge of what was actually involved, I pledged that I would one day take the journey north and hunt these high-dwelling animals in their natural habitat. Before that could happen, though, I knew I needed two things I didn't immediately have on hand: a suitable mountain rifle and enough discretionary income to book the hunt. Looking back, there were plenty of other things I should have been concerned about, but my ignorance and inexperience prevented me from considering them.

In any event, the first thing I concentrated on was the rifle. Actually, I did quite a bit of research before I settled on a Remington model 700 chambered in .300 Winchester magnum. I wanted to be sure the big-game rifle I bought was capable of killing any animal residing in North America, just in case additional hunts for other species were to grace my future. I topped the rifle with a variable-power scope, developed an accurate hand-load using 200 grain Nosler Partition bullets and did a little shooting from time to time.

Even though I now possessed a rifle fit for the task, there was no particular urgency to contract for a hunt, as the day-to-day financial and parenting demands involved in raising our two young sons forced me to categorize any prospective sheep hunt as a luxury rather than a necessity. So, several more years passed without any progress towards my dream. However, in 1988 my aunt passed away, leaving her small estate equally to me, my brother and my father. I suddenly and unexpectedly had enough cash to book my long-envisioned sheep hunt.

I knew practically nothing about the hunting industry at the time. While attending a local sportsman's show, one of the booths was manned by a booking agent who solicited clients for an outfitter operating in the Alaska Range. In an effort to attain some level of comfort with complete strangers, I'm sure I asked several cursory questions and subsequently spoke to a few of the outfitter's previous hunters. In retrospect, though, I was woefully unprepared for the task of gleaning enough relevant information to ensure a high level of confidence that I would be hunting with a reputable outfitter who could meet my needs. Actually, I spent more time and effort deciding which gun to buy than I did choosing the people who would be responsible for my welfare and the success of my hunt! It's often said that ignorance is bliss. If that's true, then I'm sure the 1988 edition of Webster's Dictionary contains my likeness alongside the definition of 'ignorance.'

Whether I had performed the appropriate due diligence or not, I was headed to the Alaska Range in September 1989 to finally see what hunting sheep was really like. Little did I know that this supposed once-in-a-lifetime hunt would be merely the first act in a long string of sheep-hunting adventures spanning more than two decades. There was no way could I have anticipated how one sheep hunt would eventually change my life in so many positive ways.

What follows are un-embellished accounts of each of my sheep hunts, whether an animal was taken or not, recreated substantially from the contemporaneous diary entries I made while I was in the mountains. I present these stories in chronological order in the hope that the reader is able to see the hunts as more than a series of (hopefully) entertaining but unconnected events. Like any multi-year endeavor, the participant can't help but evolve as the years slip by. This growth is evidenced by an increase of knowledge, greater capabilities, insights born of experience and changing goals. My journey as a sheep hunter follows this common path, and it begins now.

Dall Sheep—1989

While my primary interest was my dreamed-about Dall ram, my contract with outfitter George Palmer allowed for other animals to be harvested once the sheep had been taken. His area in the Alaska Range also held trophy Alaska-Yukon moose, as well as caribou and grizzly bear. With two weeks of actual hunting days scheduled, coming home with three animals was a distinct possibility according to everyone I spoke to.

With the hunt booked and paid for and all the travel arrangements completed, the remaining task was to wait for summer to pass. This wasn't particularly easy, as patience doesn't happen to be one of my virtues. Besides, excitement and anticipation were steadily building as the days and weeks ticked by. A week or so before the hunt a random thought crossed my mind: Perhaps I wasn't in good enough shape to handle the hunt. In order to settle my newfound unease, I decided to prove my capability by taking a long walk. Donning shorts and sneakers I made a six-mile loop near my home, staying on paved road the entire time. "There, nothing to worry about," I thought to myself as I arrived back at our driveway.

From where I sit today, this lackadaisical approach to hunt preparation seems astounding! At that time, though, I was only thirty-six years old, I wasn't carrying any extra body weight and I kept in pretty good shape doing jobs around the house. I felt I could handle anything Alaska threw at me. Although I may not have appreciated it then, I was taking a huge gamble: I was betting that my existing physical condition wouldn't jeopardize the outcome of my dream hunt. Only time would tell if my wager would prove to be foolhardy.

Prepared or not, I began my journey on September 4th, arriving by plane in Anchorage later the same day. The plan was to stay overnight in a local hotel and fly into the hunting area the next day. While at the hotel, I met two brothers from Pennsylvania who were also clients of Mr. Palmer. Like me, this was their first trip to Alaska and we were all looking forward to the scenic grandeur and the hunts which were now just beyond our reach. Unfortunately, the notorious Alaska weather would dominate the next several days, severely testing our patience in the process.

The weather around Anchorage wasn't bad, but the mountain passes which served as the door to the hunting area couldn't be safely navigated with the light aircraft used by our outfitter to ferry clients. After two of the dullest days I've ever experienced, the seemingly endless weather dilemma was finally solved by chartering a flight to McGrath on a plane with instrument-flight capability. Once in McGrath, George could fly us to the main camp at Mystic Lake with no mountain passes to contend with. The cost of the charter flight, however, fell to the prospective hunters, adding insult to the injury of the past few days. However, coughing up the cash for the flight was far preferable to another hour spent waiting in town.

George was there waiting for us when we arrived in McGrath. We loaded up the plane and headed towards the mountains. The flight may have been a feast to the eyes, but my stomach had a notably less enjoyable experience. Air turbulence caused an almost incessant buffeting, along with the occasional, sudden six-foot drop in elevation. Just before we landed my stomach finally revolted and I vomited. The guides waiting for us at the gravel airstrip at Mystic Lake must have gotten a good laugh as I literally crawled out of the plane. No matter how bad I felt at the moment, I was thrilled to finally be in the hunting area and the scenery was as awesome as I had expected.

The facilities at Mystic Lake were surprisingly comfortable given the remoteness of the location. A log lodge served as headquarters, with Mt. McKinley and Mt. Foraker visible approximately fifty air miles away. I had assumed my luck would change with the move to base camp, but I was mistaken. For the next two days high winds prevented me from being flown out to my sheep-hunting locale. Talk about frustration: I had been in Alaska a total of five full days and I hadn't even started hunting yet! These were days which were steadily being subtracted from my available hunting time. It was beginning to seem like I'd never catch a break. As we waited for a window in the weather suitable for flying, my guide-to-be, Chip Barker, and I passed the time with short walks around the adjoining hills and camp chores. I pestered him with questions about the local flora and fauna and our long-anticipated sheep hunt.

On September 10th, Chip and I were finally flown into the mountains, along with meat packer Jeff Baird. Alaska law prohibits hunting on the same day one flies in an airplane. Even though we couldn't shoot anything, at least we were finally in sheep country. In fact, we saw lots of sheep nearby, some of which were rams. To finally view in person the animal which, years ago, had inspired this journey was a special moment.

The three of us would be enjoying a traditional backpack sheep hunt, where a portable tent would serve as our shelter and we'd lug our personal gear and enough food for four days. The advantage of this type of hunt was flexibility—we could go anywhere our legs would carry us in search of sheep. On the negative side, our exposure to inclement weather was greater than if we had a small cabin or wall tent as a base of operations. Plus, backpacking requires more effort due to the fact that everything you might possibly need must be hauled around with you. As one might expect, our food was not quite what you'd find at home. Instead, packets of oatmeal and freeze-dried dinners were the norm, in order to minimize the weight we would be carrying. If we out-hunted our initial food supply, George would find us in the plane and drop off more. The plentiful glacier-fed streams would provide an unlimited supply of pristine drinking water.

In fact, waterways were so prevalent that ankle-fit hip boots were recommended footwear. This would be the first and only time I hunted sheep wearing these contraptions. Even though they proved less-than-ideal for climbing, they weren't a bad choice given the number of stream crossings we were forced to make each day. Besides the boots, my outfitter's essential equipment list specified a backpack. Unfortunately, no other detail about the pack's construction or carrying capacity was offered. Left to my own devices, which didn't include the good sense to ask for guidance and the belief that this would likely be my only sheep hunt, I borrowed a pack from a friend. This particular pack had no hip belt, so the weight would be carried entirely on my shoulders. That may have been the way the old-timers did things, but a good hip belt would have made for less-tiring packing.

It may have been a long time in the making, but shortly after leaving the makeshift airstrip on a hill at the base of a mountain, I received my initiation into mountain hunting. Chip, Jeff and I were starting from the foothills, which constituted the extreme outer fringe of sheep habitat. We needed to get back into the peaks where the big boys resided, and that meant we had to gain some elevation before side-hilling around the mountain's flank into the next drainage. The mountain was steep and it didn't take long to work up a pretty good sweat. I knew how wet I was from the effort, and I thought, "If I look at these guys and there's not a bead of perspiration on their faces, then I'm in real trouble!" Almost afraid to glance at my companions, I was relieved to find they weren't having it any easier than me.

The country was grand. The mountains were steep and tall, with about 1,500 feet of elevation separating valley floor from the peaks. The three of us were already well above the timber line and only the creek bottoms contained vegetation of any height, where willows and alders combined to form nearly impenetrable thickets. Just above this zone of brush the landscape transformed to a mat of low-growing weeds and grasses, giving the side slopes a pretty mix of crimson and yellow coloration. This ground cover began to peter out about half way up the sides of the mountains. From this uneven boundary to the top nothing grew. The exposed crowns of the mountains were black in color, consisting of a mix of gravel and hard outcroppings. Some of the highest peaks were shrouded in snow and ice. Visible lines crisscrossed the dark shale. These were sheep trails—wilderness highways used by sheep to get from one place to another for generations. I had been drawn to Alaska, at least in part, for the visual beauty the state offered, and I surely wasn't disappointed!

Once safely in the next drainage, my companions found a good campsite and set up the tent. For the rest of that day and all of the next we looked over the adjoining country for rams. The mountains were close enough to each other that the best hunting tactic was to gain elevation then walk the ridgelines, stopping often to glass into the basins on our left and our right as they came into view. During our excursions we covered quite a bit of country, some with our feet but more with our eyes. All told, we spied a couple different groups of rams but neither band contained a specimen deemed big enough to shoot. We also had the pleasure of an even rarer sighting—a lone wolf loping along 400 yards in front of us.

Although the hunt started in sunshine, it wasn't long before rain became a constant and decidedly unwelcome companion. The rain wasn't continuous but we spent a lot of time dealing with it. When we weren't huddled in our rain gear, it seemed as though we were either putting it on or taking it off. We also had to take extra precautions to keep key pieces of gear, like sleeping bags, dry. Besides those problems, the inclement weather inhibited me from enjoying my surroundings to the fullest extent possible.

After two days spent exploring the immediate area, Chip, Jeff and I decided to relocate our camp in an effort to find the right ram. Several miles on foot, including a climb over a high saddle in the mountain, and we were situated in a different drainage. With the change in location came renewed hope for success. We had been hunting hard and the effort required to traverse the steep mountain sides was considerable. Climbing in the ever-present gravel was especially tough. Oftentimes, a step up would gain no elevation, as the newly disturbed gravel would slump downward at the same time, leaving me with the sense that I was walking in place. This sheep hunting was definitely not easy! In my diary I compared the experience to paying the Marines to let me attend boot camp, just so I could be beaten up day after day. Whatever my private thoughts, I didn't dare speak of my self-doubts and fatigue to Chip and Jeff.

The next morning, we headed to a good glassing spot in the hope that we would catch a group of rams feeding before they bedded for the day. To be honest, if they were within your field of vision, you could easily distinguish the white sheep against the darker backgrounds, even without binoculars. In addition, movement always caught the eye, especially along the skyline. Due to features of the terrain, however, it was possible that sheep could be bedded nearby but invisible to probing eyes. Locating rams while they were up and about was a good way of increasing our chances of success.

The three of us had been searching the surrounding countryside for about an hour when I noticed several sheep in the same place where a single ewe had been spotted earlier. Chip put the spotting scope on the newfound animals. This time, seven rams filled his scope, including one "shooter" ram. Obviously, these rams had been hidden by a fold in the mountain and they only became visible to us as they worked their way higher. The hunt, at long last, was on!

To get to the sheep we first had to cross into the adjoining drainage. Once there, the plan was to go around the back of the mountain the rams were bedded on, and then climb above them. This was the only feasible way to approach within rifle range for the following reasons: Sheep have fabulous eyesight and they tend to employ a group defense against predators. Bedding locations are chosen with care atop a suitable promontory. In addition, individual members of the group vary their orientation so that every conceivable approach from below can be seen by at least one group member. For sheep, danger from natural enemies rarely came from above.

Our stalk wasn't without incident, nor was it straightforward. We closed to within 500 yards of the rams but a solitary ewe prevented a closer approach along the path we had chosen. Working around the ewe proved more difficult than expected, as we soon encountered a section of rocks that was too dangerous to climb through. Unfortunately, this treacherous patch extended all the way to the top of the mountain, forcing us to give up a lot of hard-earned elevation, traverse below the obstacle, and then re-climb to our previous altitude. From there, though, the climb to the top proceeded without further difficulty. When we crept forward and peered over the crest of the ridge, four of the rams were visible directly below us, bedded only 150 yards away. It was a pretty sight, but the ram we were after was tucked behind a rocky outcropping out of our view.

For the entire stalk, I could feel the tension steadily building as we slowly closed the distance. In part, this was due to the uncertainty of the situation. The rams were out of our sight for most of the stalk; there was no guarantee they'd stay put while we struggled to get to them; and even if they remained in place, we couldn't be confident they'd be accessible for a shot once we reached our perch. As it turned out, due to vagaries of the topography, the band of rams was about one-half accessible. Adding to the anxiety caused by these unknowns was my own battle with performance pressure. Obviously, this hunt was very important to me. The hunt was years in the making, I had traveled far, worked extremely hard and spent a considerable amount of money just to have the opportunity that was apparently getting closer with each step. Ultimately, my success would likely be determined by my ability to execute when I was presented with a shooting opportunity.

With the only mature ram in the group hidden away, our best option was to wait for a change in circumstance. Bedded sheep routinely get up, mill around and assume different positions during the day, even within a bedding location. Plus, if they began to feed in earnest we would likely have a reasonable shot opportunity, even if it meant we had to move. The sheep didn't know we were there, we held the high ground and we could use the available cover to mask our movements.

After nearly an hour of unremarkable surveillance, a change in fortune came quickly and without warning. The wind had been favorable, as the day's warming kept the thermal wind currents rising from the sheep to us. For a moment, the wind changed and one of the younger rams stood and tipped his nose skyward. In a flash, the entire group was up and running towards our left. Abandoning most of our gear, the three of us ran across the relatively flat crest in an attempt to intercept the fleeing rams. We saw them, but they were too far away and moving too quickly to even contemplate taking a shot. It seemed as though all was lost as the sheep put more ground between them and us. Everyone was stunned at what had just transpired!

The sheep were headed across the side of a contiguous mountain, about two-thirds of the way to the top. As we gulped air to replenish the oxygen lost in our sprint, and before any real disappointment could sink in, the sheep disappeared into a narrow ravine which ran vertically up the mountainside. When they failed to come out on the far side of the depression, we figured they were following the cut towards the top. We were standing in a saddle abutting a ridge on the same mountain the sheep were on. I immediately noticed that the ridgeline and the ravine converged as they ascended, as well as the potential benefit this quirk of terrain offered. Assuming we could reach the same elevation in time, it looked as though the sheep might be within range as they emerged from the cut.

It may have been the longest of long shots, but racing the sheep to the top was our only remaining chance to get that ram. If the odds makers in Las Vegas were to handicap our chances of success, 100-1 odds would have been generous! Hopeless or not, I just wasn't willing to let that ram get away without trying. We had come too far and worked too hard to give up now.

Almost without hesitation the three of us began climbing along the ridgeline as fast as we could, with me in the lead. We had already spent a great deal of energy just getting to where the sheep had been bedded, and what little reserves we had remaining were rapidly bleeding away as we ascended. Time was of the essence so we pushed on despite the fatigue, and soon we were high enough that we had snow beneath our feet. We had climbed hundreds of feet in a matter of minutes. Just as the sheep began filing out of the ravine we arrived at the same topographical contour on the ridge, gasping for breath. Although I wasn't sure what the exact range was, I heard Chip say, "You can kill him from here." The rams were walking slowly, having long since put us out of their minds. Our collective best estimate placed the rams a little over 300 yards away.

My biggest problem was getting into a steady shooting position. I hastily assumed a sitting position using a large rock as a rest. Still, my oxygen-starved lungs were causing rapid breathing and my heart was pounding, both of which resulted in the cross hairs of my scope bouncing all over the sheep. My first shot was a clean miss but I collected myself and the second shot hit the ram in the hindquarters, stopping him in his tracks. One final round through the lungs took the ram's life and he collapsed, rolling back into the ravine and out of sight. I had my sheep!

A sense of relief was the first emotion I felt, followed by happiness and satisfaction. I think we were all too exhausted to really savor the moment, though Chip and Jeff made it clear to me that this wasn't normally the way sheep hunts ended; this was special. It was now about 4pm and it took us nearly forty-five minutes to get to the ram, which couldn't have been in a worse spot. Pictures were impossible, as our cameras had been left far below in our haste to chase the sheep. Because it was so late in the day, Chip decided the best course of action was to gut the ram, take the head and enough hide for a shoulder mount, and descend to the valley. We would retrieve the rest of our gear en route, and Jeff would climb back up the next morning to collect the meat. Five hours later, just as darkness was descending, we arrived at the creek bed, totally spent from the day's effort.

Jeff and Chip set up camp and prepared some supper. I was so exhausted I didn't dare eat anything for fear of being sick.

The three of us had hardly entered the tent when it began to rain, and it poured all night. Sleep was a scarce commodity. By morning, though, the rain had petered out. As Jeff climbed back to the kill site to recover the meat, Chip and I had a chance to admire the ram. Several inches of the left horn were missing, most likely the result of a previous battle for breeding rights. The right horn looked like a corkscrew—over forty inches in length and approximately one-quarter past full curl. He was obviously an older ram and we were able to count eleven annual rings (circumferential interruptions in horn growth that occur during winter), making the ram $11^1/_2$ years old. To this day, that distinguishes him as the oldest ram I've ever taken.

The new day also brought with it an unusual reminder of the previous day's extreme sheep chase. My throat was sore, although not in the conventional sense. Instead of the lining being irritated, it was the muscles surrounding my windpipe which were sore. This feeling, the result of the rapid and exaggerated breathing pattern exhibited during our prolonged race up the mountain, would last for several days. Never before had I experienced such a sensation, nor has it been replicated since that day, giving testament to the uniqueness of the endeavor.

Once Jeff returned we started our march to lower elevations. We first had to climb over a saddle into the next drainage. From there, our destination was a cabin located at the point where the creek we stood next to emptied into another stream, a dozen miles downstream. Even though the walking was over relatively level ground, it wasn't particularly easy. We all had heavy packs and we were forced to repeatedly cross the creek in order to avoid stretches where the river hugged sheer side banks. It rained for most of the trip and the persistent rain of the past several days had swollen the waterway, making for some treacherous crossings. Nevertheless, we finally arrived at the cabin around 7pm, tired and wet.

When most people hear the word 'oasis' they picture a green, fertile island surrounded by sand. For three hungry, exhausted and drenched sheep hunters, the cabin at the river junction was as welcome as a sip of water to the man dying of thirst in the desert. Good food, dry clothes and a roof over our heads were rewards for our ordeal in the mountains. Chip and I would spend the next several days hunting moose from this cabin (Jeff's presence was needed elsewhere), and despite continuing bad weather we eventually took a very good bull.

My first sheep hunt had been a success—an exceptional Dall ram was now in my possession. I had overcome horrible weather and I had acquitted myself well in the eyes of my guides, earning their respect. But I wasn't happy! Without doubt, the dismal weather put a damper on the overall experience, impeding my ability to enjoy the majesty of my surroundings. Beyond that, though, the sheep hunting had been pure torture, even though we had only spent three full days in its practice. When I left Alaska, and for a long time thereafter, I doubted I would ever feel the need to hunt sheep again.

After many days of waiting, I was finally able to begin my hunt. This photo was taken shortly after landing at the base of this mountain. The two white dots in the center of the shot are Dall rams—my first sighting of my quarry.

This shot was taken from one of the numerous streams we had to navigate during the hunt.

After gaining some altitude, the grandeur of the setting becomes more apparent.

My very first wild sheep—a Dall ram from the Alaska Range.
Photo by Chip Barker

STONE SHEEP—1990

Subsequent to my Alaska trip my feelings about the hunt began to slowly shift. The pain and suffering, not to mention the pall cast by the inclement weather, began to fade in importance. At the same time, the positive aspects of the hunt assumed a more prominent place. The passage of time allowed me to re-evaluate those events with the benefit of perspective. Perhaps the best analogy is childbirth: In the moments leading up to the birth, pain dominates a woman's consciousness; after the child is born, however, joy eclipses discomfort. My transformation was also helped by the attention I received from my family and hunting buddies, as I frequently found myself detailing the trip in words, pictures and by the display of my coveted sheep horns.

Sometime during this transition I began to better inform myself about sheep hunting. I learned that there were four species of wild sheep inhabiting North America: Dall, Stone, bighorn and desert bighorn. I also discovered that the taking of all four of these sheep comprised something called the Grand Slam®. In sheep-hunting circles, this was considered a major accomplishment. Apparently, hunters who had achieved such a feat were few in number and they occupied an exalted place within the larger hunting community.

I'd be lying if I said that belonging to such an exclusive club didn't appeal to my vain side, but the prospect seemed highly unlikely and I certainly wasn't obsessed with the attainment of this particular goal. Nevertheless, I did make some inquires about Stone sheep hunts, checking out a couple of outfitters in the process. In the end, I decided not to book a hunt with anyone, as I had an elk hunt planned in the fall with my father. Plus, Stone sheep hunts were much more expensive than my Dall hunt had been, and I was still ambivalent about sheep hunting in general.

Much to my surprise, I received a call during the last week of July from one of the outfitters I had researched. Art Thompson of Gundahoo River Outfitters in northern British Columbia had a cancellation and wanted to know if I could be there by the first of August. The discounted cost of the hunt was incentive enough to drop everything, rearrange my schedule and buy a plane ticket. The encouragement of an understanding wife sealed the deal!

Because I booked my flights at the last minute, my itinerary left something to be desired, but four planes later I arrived in Ft. Nelson at the appointed time. Art and his wife Crystal were there to meet me, but my rifle had taken a detour somewhere along the way. That was upsetting, but Art assured me my gun would eventually catch up to me. Besides, I could use one of his guns if my rifle wasn't immediately forthcoming. With nothing left to do, we headed up the Alaska Highway, arriving at the Thompson's lodge located at beautiful, copper-blue Muncho Lake some three hours after leaving the airport.

All outfitters have a base of operations which acts as a clearinghouse for incoming and outgoing clients. Depending upon the circumstances, an outfitter's home or wall tents in the bush can serve the purpose. More times than not, though, a lodge with outbuildings within the hunting area is the hub of the outfitting wheel. Sleeping quarters, a kitchen, running water to wash the stench off of hunters returning from the field and a phone for the inevitable calls to home and the airlines are the main requirements of such a facility.

Sheds to store tools, supplies and horse tack are welcome and useful amenities. Whatever configuration this base of operation takes, it will reflect the needs and desires of the outfitter conducting the hunts. Art and Crystal's facility was comfortable and well-suited for the sheep, moose and mountain goat hunts they provided.

We didn't have a lot of time to waste, as Art had a schedule to keep and the first legal hunting day (August 1st) was already lost. In fact, our sheep camp had already been prepared and was currently being manned by native guide Alfred Stone, who was waiting for us to arrive. For the time being, at least, I was the outfit's first and only client of the new hunting season. Besides Alfred, Art and his son Quentin would accompany me on the hunt. With this many people attending to me and to the success of my hunt, how could we possibly fail?

Early the next morning we prepared for the horse ride into the high country. Since my rifle hadn't arrived during the night, I had to select one of Art's guns. I chose his Remington model 700 in 7mm magnum caliber because it most closely mirrored my rifle in both ballistics and operation. Once the gun was zeroed, we loaded the truck and horse trailer for the ten-mile ride up the highway. The four Stone sheep we saw standing in the road during the trip only reinforced my belief that the hunt would go well. Arriving at our demarcation point, any horses which weren't saddled for human transport were packed with supplies and the entire pack train headed for camp.

Art, Quentin and I had a good trail to follow and as we climbed higher, we stopped to glass for sheep on occasion. The mountains in this part of British Columbia were much different than those in Alaska. Although they were comparable in regards to vertical relief, steepness and elevation (5,000-7,000 feet), the mountains here were, in a word, verdant. Plant life was much more common than it had been in Alaska. Evergreen trees dominated the valleys and extended well up onto the mountain sides. From there, a zone of alders, willows and buck brush formed a higher belt of green. Grasses grew from the top of the brush all the way to the peaks, as well as dominating the numerous avalanche slides. There, the violence of cascading snow had obliterated the trees and opened the canopy to sunshine. The mountain tops weren't universally green, as rocky outcroppings and dry washes interrupted zones of plant life. The resultant panorama was one of exceptional beauty.

Early August at this northern latitude was characterized by two other natural phenomena: one a blessing; the other a curse. The days enjoyed a decisive advantage over the nights. There was light enough to see (and hunt) for almost twenty hours out of each full day. Even the shortened period of darkness was muted somewhat, as it never really became pitch black. All that daylight, accompanied by moderate temperatures, made for an ideal breeding ground for the various biting insects native to the area. And bite they did! It was a full-time job shoeing the pests away, and even then, I wasn't 100% successful in my efforts.

The three of us made it to camp with daylight to spare, enjoyed a good meal and turned in for the night, full of anticipation for what the next day might bring. Alfred had located a good ram not too far from camp and we expected to focus our attention in that direction when the new day dawned. By 5am Alfred, Art and I were headed to the basin where the ram was last seen. Quentin stayed in camp. After a couple of hours of fairly easy climbing, we were well-positioned to scour the mountain sides for signs of sheep.

While it had been relatively easy to spot Dall sheep in Alaska against their dark backgrounds, finding Stone sheep was another matter. Stone sheep vary in color from almost all white to very dark. Most animals exhibit a salt-and-pepper mixture that blends very well with the surrounding terrain, making them very difficult to pick out, especially in rocky settings. When the sheep fed, however, movement would help give them away, especially if they were facing away from you. In this presentation, the white rumps and white backs of the legs gave the unmistakable appearance of an upside-down 'V' to anyone looking at their backside. Even then, it took a trained eye and lots of patience to consistently find these beautiful animals.

We had been glassing for some time when Art spotted a sheep crossing the face of the basin. Shortly thereafter, more sheep appeared. Eventually, with the assistance of a spotting scope, a total of ten rams traveling together were identified, including two potential shooters. We waited to see where they bedded for the day before planning our next moves. At 10:30am, reasonably confident the rams would stay put for awhile, we carefully backed out of the basin and began our stalk up the opposite side of the ridge the rams occupied.

Following the normal tactic when hunting sheep, we intended to close the distance to within reasonable shooting range using the ridge to shield our movements, and then pop back over to the sheep's side of the mountain. With a little luck, we'd find ourselves above the clueless rams in a good position to take the shot. The stalk went well, but in places the footing was a little scary. In one spot we had to traverse a narrow ledge below a sheer vertical rock face, and at another location we squeezed through a one-foot-wide crevice in solid stone. Eventually, we closed the distance sufficiently and traversed the mountain's spine. Using a side ridge off the main ridge for concealment, we carefully crawled to within 225 yards of the still-bedded rams.

Our newfound proximity allowed us to evaluate the two good rams more thoroughly than before. One ram could be identified by his very wide horns, dark body and gray face. In addition, there was a very distinctive dark marking in the shape of a diamond in the middle of the ram's nose. The other ram had a white face and horns that were narrower than but just as impressive as those worn by the first ram. After much discussion, the consensus settled on taking the wide ram. We would have to wait for him to stand up, so I'd have the entire vital zone to aim at.

As in my previous hunt, anticipation of the moment when I would pull the trigger had been building for the entire stalk. The hunt in Alaska had ended abruptly, though, without much time to really think about the shot. This time, I was confronted with the additional burden of a protracted wait before I could perform the singular duty which could determine the outcome of the hunt. Psychologically, this self-imposed pressure was not an easy thing to deal with, especially with the ram so teasingly close by. Years later, I would utilize coping mechanisms to help me deal with these situations more effectively, but those tools weren't yet in my bag of tricks. I did my best to remain calm, but I was only partially successful.

It may have seemed like an eternity, but within the hour the ram finally stood to stretch. Although my body position was uncomfortable—a common occurrence in mountain settings—the sights seemed steady as I pulled the trigger. Art called the shot 'high' before I had recovered from the recoil. All the rams jumped to their feet as I chambered another round. Holding a little lower, I shot again and the ram dropped! I had felt the effects of adrenalin in my system before the shot, but its influence was even more pronounced in the wake of the ram's demise, as the pent-up tension dissipated and my hands began to shake. All three of us couldn't have been more pleased with the outcome as we exchanged kudos. A quick glance at my watch showed the hour to be 1:30pm. It had taken less than nine hours of actual hunting to shoot a beautiful Stone ram.

The remaining sheep still hadn't discovered our whereabouts. Wishing not to disturb them, we patiently waited while they slowly climbed out of the basin, leaving their fallen comrade behind. After thirty minutes we approached the downed ram. For me, there's always a little sadness mingling amongst the euphoria that comes with the purposeful death of a big-game animal. The ram was every bit as good as Art and Alfred had estimated him to be: the bases were heavy with horn lengths of 40 and 37 inches.

We took lots of pictures before removing the cape, horns and meat. Art would carry the horns on his shoulders and Alfred was to pack all the meat. During our initial descent from the ram's high resting place, Alfred was navigating a narrow shelf in the rocks, dragging his heavy pack behind him, when he lost his balance. He let go of the pack to save himself from falling and it tumbled down towards Art and me, spilling its contents as it bounced. Two sheep quarters literally landed at my feet. Clearly, Alfred's shredded backpack was no longer capable of transporting all the meat. I was wearing a small daypack that Art had lent me, and although there wasn't any spare room inside, the pack did have an external haul loop at the top. By passing a rope through this loop and securing the knuckle of each hind quarter on either end of the rope, we cobbled together a way to transport half of the meat.

Normally, three healthy men with good backpacks would have had a pretty easy time carrying out a sheep. After Alfred's mishap, though, there wasn't a decent pack in the entire group. Consequently, the trip back to camp wasn't easy for any of us. Certainly, I had problems: some of my own making and some due to circumstances beyond my control. Understandably, the meat would swing back and forth as I descended, making it difficult to maintain my balance. Besides that, all the weight was transmitted to my shoulders, and not very efficiently at that. The second issue was my footwear. Because the hunt had been taken on extremely short notice, I didn't have a good pair of hunting boots suitable for the mountains. I suppose I could have worn the ankle-fit hip boots I had worn the previous year, but I thought the general-purpose work boots I owned would get me through the hunt.

The further we went the more my feet deteriorated. Foot movement within the boot, exacerbated by the extra weight, was causing major blistering. Eventually, the blisters burst, leaving raw, oozing and even more painful sores. I made it most of the way back to camp before I succumbed to the pain and the weariness, and asked to be relieved of my load. Art bore the extra burden without complaint as I hustled forward to seek Quentin's help. All things considered, I had done pretty well. After all, at the outset I hadn't been expected to carry a thing. However, to this day, I regret not toughing it out, even if it meant limping into camp with blood-soaked socks. I also shudder to think of what might have happened if the hunt had lasted several days instead of just a few hours.

Quentin was pleased to hear of our success when I reached him and he quickly scurried back up the game trail to assist his dad. More than fifteen eventful hours after we had departed, everyone was back in camp, basking in the glory of the day. Of course, the first order of business was to devour enough food and drink to replace our depleted reserves. With our stomachs full, sleep came very easily.

We spent most of the next day in the mountains before riding out to the highway later in the afternoon. The day couldn't have been nicer weather-wise. The highlight, though, was the sight of a band of more than a dozen rams bedded at the very top of a peak across from camp. I spent a couple more days at the lodge on Muncho Lake before returning home. Fortunately, my rifle had arrived during our absence. One night we took a trip up the highway to the Liard River hot springs, a very well-kept and attractive Provincial Park. The sultry water had the unmistakable smell of sulfur and soaking in it performed wonders on my aching muscles, not to mention my numerous bug bites. Years later, this same park would gather international attention as the scene of a black bear attack where one person was killed and others injured.

Besides being a consummate host and outfitter, Art introduced me to an organization called the Foundation for North American Wild Sheep (now the Wild Sheep Foundation). I hadn't known that there was a group dedicated to protecting and improving the plight of sheep and their habitat. Upon returning home, I promptly joined the ranks and attended their annual convention the following January. For a neophyte sheep hunter, the convention proved to be an invaluable source of information about sheep, outfitters and hunting gear. I've been a proud member of the Foundation ever since, and I've met many wonderful, like-minded people along the way.

In many ways, my sheep hunt in British Columbia had been everything my hunt in Alaska had not been: short, enjoyable and rain free. In fact, I had spent eight days in Alaska either sitting around waiting to hunt or hunting before I eventually shot my sheep; if my Stone sheep hunt was dated to Art's initial phone call the hunt durations were comparable, even though I spent much of the time home. I guess things tend to even out over time. One thing was certain: The positive experience in Canada, reinforced by my subsequent attendance at the FNAWS convention, made it more likely that sheep hunting would be a part of my future.

As I reflected upon my two hunts, I realized I really hadn't been adequately prepared for either. Sure, I had two great rams but I hadn't put any effort into training my body for the rigorous demands of the mountains. Besides that deficiency, I lacked at least two critical pieces of equipment every sheep hunter should have: a well-constructed backpack and boots specifically designed for mountain hunting. I vowed that if I were to go sheep hunting again, I wouldn't do so unless I had taken steps to correct both of these shortcomings.

Muncho Lake on the Alaska Highway north of Ft. Nelson, British Columbia. Gundahoo River Outfitters has its base of operations located at the northern end of this body of water.

The natural beauty of northern British Columbia. In early August, everything from valley floor to mountain top was green.

This Stone ram, my second sheep overall, has very wide horns. Notice also, the dark diamond-shaped coloration on the ram's nose.

DALL SHEEP—1991

Sometime after my hunt in British Columbia, probably at the FNAWS convention, I obtained a promotional catalog from a company called Wild Wings. They produced and sold limited-edition wildlife art. One of the items in the publication was an art print which really caught my eye. A work by artist Ron Van Gilder titled, "High Trails—Dall Sheep," featured three Dall rams standing on a ridge and looking towards the viewer. The caption below the image described the setting as the Chugach Mountains of Alaska. Although the print was very nice, it was the ruggedness of the terrain which piqued my interest. I thought to myself, "That looks like a real tough place to hunt," and filed the information away for future consideration.

As things stood, I was half way to achieving a Grand Slam®, and for the first time, I gave serious thought to its achievement. Many slammers start the same way I had and progress directly to the two remaining species. It's not unusual for hunts to be spaced years apart, though. Sometimes these self-imposed interruptions provide a mechanism to save for the next hunt; at other times the hunter is hoping to draw a coveted permit in the western United States. I knew that prices for bighorn and desert sheep hunts were much higher than hunts for Dall sheep. If sheep hunting was to become a regular part of my life, simple math indicated I could get more bang for my buck by making Dalls my objective. In other words, I could go hunting more often if I forgot about becoming a slammer and concentrated instead on the cheaper-to-hunt white sheep.

As my thinking consolidated along these lines, I reckoned back to the previous image of the Chugach Mountains and the challenge they seemed to pose. Once I decided to hunt sheep again, I intentionally sought out a guide/outfitter who hunted there. While searching, I came across an advertisement for Last Frontier Guiding & Outfitting, owned by Rocky Keen. After speaking to him over the phone and checking his references, I booked a hunt for mid-August.

This hunt, in contrast to the previous two, would find me better prepared for the mountains. I purchased a backpack and a good pair of mountain boots. More important, I did a lot of walking wearing both in the months leading up to the hunt. When August arrived, the boots were broken-in and my body was strong from many miles spent carrying extra weight in the pack.

As promised, Rocky met me at the airport in Anchorage. On this occasion, none of my luggage was missing. We drove several hours north to Glennallen, where Rocky stowed his airplane at a gravel airstrip built just for smaller planes. The short flight into his camp was pretty but somewhat bumpy. Fortunately, the trip hadn't lasted long enough to make me sick. Rocky's base camp consisted of a simple wood building located in a picturesque valley at a place where the timber was just beginning to thin out due to the elevation.

Two of Rocky's guides greeted us as we exited the plane. Jeff Douglas would shepherd me on my hunt, while Larry Spiva had just come into camp with a sheep one of his hunters had killed. Larry's clients were still in the mountains and he planned to return to their camp after a brief rest. The ram was very impressive, causing me to become a little more excited about my prospects. Out of curiosity I asked Larry his hunter's name. He replied, "Ron Van Gilder." My head snapped as I quickly responded, "The artist?" I subsequently made it clear that I didn't know Mr. Van Gilder personally but I was aware of his work. "Boy, that's an amazing coincidence," I thought to myself.

The next day, Jeff and I walked three hours up the valley in the rain to our spike camp, a comfortable tent-like structure supported by curved aluminum ribs. Later in the day the rain abated and we were able to do some glassing. In all, we spotted more than a dozen lambs and ewes but no rams could be found.

One thing was for sure: this definitely wasn't the Alaska Range. Approximately half of what I was viewing at any given time couldn't be climbed. Without technical climbing gear—and the experience to use it safely—large sections of the surrounding mountains were off-limits to humans. That was one difference; the other was the low blanket of green growth that extended to the highest reaches. To me, these two factors suggested that the smartest rams could die of old age without ever exposing themselves to hunters. If they wished, rams could simply remain among the inaccessible pinnacles and still find enough food to survive.

Jeff and I were up very early the next morning for what would prove to be one of the most eventful days I ever spent hunting sheep, especially considering the fact that I never even fired the gun! To begin with, there wasn't a drop of rain all day. Second, we were gone a long time and covered a lot of ground, expending a lot of energy in the process. Our day started at 4am and we returned to the port-a-tent in the dark at 11pm, the northern lights flickering in the black sky for the last hour of our journey. The approximately fifteen miles we covered on foot featured a fair amount of climbing, and one harrowing descent. The two of us saw plenty of sheep—nearly eighty in all. Most of them were lambs and ewes, but we did stalk a band of ten rams. The group probably contained three legal rams, but I was looking for something at least as good as the Dall I had taken two years ago, so we passed on them.

The country was spectacular and every bit as rugged as it had been portrayed in that print in the Wild Wings catalog. Jagged peaks, boulder fields and hanging pocket glaciers punctuated the landscape. Whereas the Alaska Range had been dominated by gravel, these mountains were extremely rocky. One basin would be lush with vegetation, but once we crossed a saddle into the next drainage, it seemed as though we were standing on the moon. The contrast between the adjoining settings couldn't have been starker. Water was plentiful. Small creeks occupied every valley and a small waterfall exited a high glacier-fed lake.

The harrowing descent I referenced earlier deserves some elaboration. Early in the day we had crossed a ridge to access the next valley. In order to do so, we had to jump across a small chasm. The leap also included a three-foot drop. That was done safely, but it was obvious the route could not be utilized for our return, as we couldn't possibly make the jump in an uphill direction. Unfortunately, the other options for coming back were few and they were also fraught with danger. After some serious thought, we chose to descend a narrow dry gully which ran to the bottom of the mountain.

I knew this was serious work before we started, but the adrenalin rush that washed over me when I entered the slide signaled not only that my conscious brain had become acutely attuned to the danger, but that there was no possibility of getting back out! Jeff had entered the danger zone first, and it didn't take long for me to realize that if I fell, in all likelihood, I would bowl him over and neither of us would come to a stop until we hit bottom. For approximately 600 vertical feet we clung to every meager knob or irregularity the predominantly smooth bedrock offered, simultaneously using both hands and both feet for support in order to prevent a fall. I don't believe I've ever concentrated so completely on a single activity in my entire life.

Jeff and I had begun this escapade late in the day and due to the imminent danger, the effort was taking much longer than we had expected. The sun was steadily sinking towards the horizon, and with it, a deadline loomed over our descent. We simply had to reach the bottom while we could still see; there was no other option which included our survival! Finally, after almost two hours, we exited the chute, mentally and physically drained from our ordeal. I silently thanked God for watching over us, as Jeff hugged me and apologized for our potentially disastrous predicament. The rest of the walk back to camp was, gratefully, unremarkable.

Most of the sheep seemed to be concentrated in the big feed bowl at the end of the valley, so we decided to leave the relative comfort of the port-a-tent and reposition our base of operations closer to the action. Doing so would save us several hours of walking each day, allowing us more time to hunt. For the rest of the hunt, the two of us would be living out of a two-man tent.

For the next several days Jeff and I explored the country proximate to the feed bowl. In the process, we observed many interesting things. While crossing a saddle we came eye to eye with a young ram at about thirty yards. He didn't quite know what to make of us, and he seemed more curious than afraid. We also walked by an immature ram which had recently died. He hadn't been there long and there were no obvious injuries that would explain his demise. Nature can be very cruel at times. Sheep trails were common, but there was one which stood out. This particular pathway angled through a field of boulders, some of which were as large as garbage cans. The trail may not have been as wide as a sidewalk through town, but it was as easy to follow. One wonders how many animals had to traverse this same ground to form a road amongst such weighty and bulky material.

The two of us saw sheep on a daily basis. The bowl always held dozens of animals, lambs and ewes mostly. One group of five rams had our attention for awhile. We stalked to within 500 yards, but after careful evaluation, I decided that the only legal ram in the band wasn't big enough to shoot. The highlight of the sheep sightings was a solitary ram we spotted at the very top of one particularly nasty mountain. If the Disney Corporation were to produce an animated film about wild sheep, the vista before us would have been used as the closing scene to the movie. The ram was spectacular and he stood like a statute at the top of the highest pinnacle in his unapproachable kingdom, proudly surveying all that was below.

The next to last day of my hunt brought with it the opportunity we had been working so diligently towards. Feeling that we had exhausted all the other nearby possibilities, Jeff and I reluctantly climbed the mountain-of-the-treacherous-descent in order to look for rams in the country beyond. Three rams were immediately visible on a distant ridge. As we evaluated them, I noticed another group of rams ascending a ridge behind and above the first band. It only took a brief look through the spotting scope to tell that a really good ram was leading the second group.

The stalk was long but it looked fairly straightforward: We could run the ridge we occupied, cross through a saddle and then climb the adjoining mountain. Once we passed beyond the 6,060-foot peak, we expected to be reasonably close to the sheep. Our approach transpired as we had expected, and we eventually had the rams an estimated 350 yards away—below us and still bedded. I really didn't want to take a shot of that length if there was a possibility of inching closer, however. After looking at the possibilities, we felt we could drop off the main ridgeline and advance to a finger ridge. If all went well, this side ridge would conceal our movements and we could shoot from it once we were there.

Our change in locations shaved about fifty yards off the shooting distance, but left me with a far-from-ideal shooting position. For hunters who've never experienced mountainous settings, it's difficult to describe some of the make-do, half-assed, pretzel-bodied, improvised shooting stances one must cob together just to get the cross hairs on target. There's just no way to replicate these kinds of circumstances at home, either, so you can't really prepare for them. Unfortunately, getting the sights on the sheep and keeping the sights on the sheep are not the same thing.

My predicament was one of the worst I have ever experienced. The incline combined with the jagged rocks caused me to struggle just to keep my place on the mountain. To make matters worse, the ram was bedded and I had to wait nearly an hour for him to stand before I could attempt a shot. During the seemingly interminable wait, my awkward stance began to induce muscle tremors in my legs.

At long last the ram stood. When I pulled the trigger the sight picture looked good. Nevertheless, for the third time in three years, my first shot resulted in a clean miss. Disturbed but not spooked, the entire group slowly walked out of sight below us. Jeff and I quickly climbed back up to the main ridge and began walking down its spine, looking for the rams on both sides as we advanced. We hadn't gone far when Jeff spotted the big ram below us, feeding with his head facing away at less than 100 yards! My carefully aimed off-hand shot immediately put him down. Any despair we felt after my misplaced initial shot was quickly replaced with the happiness that accompanied a fortuitous and successful second chance.

Fortunately, the ram had come to a quick stop when it dropped. The terrain was ragged and steep, and a couple of extra lunges by the sheep as it was dying could have resulted in a very long and precipitous ride, with the likelihood of serious horn and pelt damage. In fact, the footing was so problematic that we had trouble finding a reasonably stable place for the ram that would also allow us to safely take pictures. Speaking of the ram, he was a real beauty! The left horn measured $38 1/2$ inches around the curl, while the right horn stretched the tape to $39 3/4$ inches. The bases weren't huge ($13 1/2$), but the horns carried their mass well. I couldn't have been happier.

With the ram reduced to the essentials and loaded in our packs, we started our descent off the mountain. A heavy pack made it difficult to maintain my balance during the precarious initial leg of our journey, but we both made it to the valley without incident. Still, a gut-busting climb lay ahead. Halfway up the mountain Jeff, who was carrying substantially more weight than was I, ran out of gas. We had begun the day at 6am, killed the ram at 5pm, and it was now an hour before midnight. Since we presently occupied a decent spot of ground, we decided to stay there until daylight. I put on all my clothes and hunkered down out of the wind as best as I could.

An hour later, though, Jeff was feeling better. A nearly full moon and scarce cloud cover afforded us good visibility, so we decided to climb higher. We were on the backside of the same mountain where we had survived the previously detailed treacherous descent, now several days in the past. As we approached the top, our attention quickly began to focus on finding a way to circumvent the hazards we had encountered earlier and safely descend to our tent. There was no way we would expose ourselves to that kind of danger again, especially in the dark!

Nearing the summit, it appeared as though a short but difficult climb up a narrow chimney would do the job. But alas, upon ascending the route we discovered it was blocked from above. Jeff and I were about to turn back when I noticed another possibility. To our left, there appeared to be an alternate exit from the chimney. It was a little dicey, but we were able to carefully slide around a convex bulge in the mountain and onto a nearby sheep trail which ran down the ridgeline to a saddle. From there, it was a relatively easy walk down to our tent, which we finally reached at 2:30am, more than twenty hours after we had departed. We quickly devoured some food and then passed out in our sleeping bags.

Our decision to continue in the dark of the previous night proved to be a wise one, as it began raining shortly after our return. When we rolled out of our bags around 8am it was still misting. If we had waited for daylight, the dangerous sections of our route would have featured slick wet rocks, making the climbing more hazardous. Packing all our gear, we prepared for the ten-mile hike back to the main camp. Several tiring hours later we strode into Rocky's camp wet and hungry, our odyssey complete.

While we filled our stomachs to our heart's desire, Jeff and I recounted our hunt for Rocky's benefit. We detailed all the country we had covered and the sheep we had seen. We then described how we had accessed the area where I had killed my ram, on that day and the time prior. When Rocky realized the exact location of our harrowing descent, he just shook his head and cringed! He also raised the possibility that the gully we had entered could have led to a sheer ledge which offered no means of getting the rest of the way down. Not until I heard Rocky's words had that scary possibility even entered my mind.

Later in the day, Rocky and I flew back to the relative bustle of Glennallen. Just before takeoff, Rocky asked if I was okay. When I indicated I was fine, he powered up the Supercub's throttle and then said, "We're gone." In seconds we were airborne. Some hours after landing in Glennallen, we arrived at the Keen residence in Wasilla. That evening, Ron Van Gilder's name came up. Pulling out his signed print of "High Trails—Dall Sheep," Rocky said something startling: "That's where you got your sheep, you know." As I studied the terrain which served as the backdrop for the work, the proverbial light bulb snapped on in my head and I suddenly came to the realization that this was, indeed, the same mountain on which I had shot my ram. The 6,060-foot peak rising in the background, as well as the contiguous geography, was unmistakable. It may seem improbable, but the very painting which had inspired me to hunt the Chugach Mountains had also served as the exact backdrop to my successful hunt!

Of all the places I've ever hunted, this section of the Chugach Mountains remains at the top of my list for both rugged beauty and inherent difficulty. The fact that I was able to handle the harsh environment and endure the difficulties with relative ease marked an important personal transition: Before this hunt I was just a guy who had gone on a couple of sheep hunts; whereas at the hunt's conclusion, I had become a genuine sheep hunter. I had passed up opportunities on easier-to-kill but smaller sheep and held out for an outstanding ram. I endured blistered feet and aching muscles without complaint, and I contributed in meaningful ways to our success. I even carried the head, horns and cape of my ram those many miles from the kill site to the cabin. I had been tested and I had been up to the task. I still had a lot to learn, of course, but it felt pretty good to have elevated my sheep-hunting prowess to a higher plane.

Guide Jeff Douglas sitting atop a rather severe spine of rock leading to the mountain's peak.

Beautiful mountain scenery. The peak in the background to the right is 6,060 feet in elevation. I shot my ram on the far side of that mountain.

This is the mountain that gave us all the trouble crossing from the backside to this side. Our treacherous descent took place in one of the narrow shadowed gullies just to the right of the picture's center.

An outstanding Dall ram from the Chugach Mountains of Alaska. I may look at ease, but I'm precariously positioned and hanging on for dear life.
Photo by Jeff Douglas

ROCKY MOUNTAIN BIGHORN SHEEP—
1992

One of the advantages of being a member of FNAWS was the opportunity to attend their annual convention each winter. Besides having a chance to check out the numerous sheep outfitters who maintained booths at the show, I could also compare notes with other hunters. If something interested me, there were brochures, newsletters and other promotional materials I could pick up for later review. My wife and I were also developing an ever-increasing circle of friends. Outfitters with whom I had previously hunted, like the Keens and the Thompsons, as well as some of their other clients formed this core group. But, Janet and I met new and interesting people all the time.

  I really hadn't made a decision whether to hunt sheep in 1992, although I was always vacuuming up tidbits of information in the hope that something worthwhile might come my way and guide my thinking. A discussion with another sheep hunter led me to my next hunt, and it wouldn't be for Dall sheep despite my economic rationale of the previous year. Glowing reports about Alberta bighorn outfitter Nayda Hallett, combined with the comparatively low cost of the hunt, renewed my interest in pursuing a Grand Slam® of sheep. When I returned home from the convention, I immediately called Ms. Hallett and subsequently booked a hunt for September.

Technically, there are two sub-species of bighorn sheep—California bighorns and Rocky Mountain bighorns. I was to hunt the latter. I assumed there was little difference, except maybe coloration, between bighorn sheep and the two sheep species I had hunted already. Although I was too green to know it at the time, I couldn't have been more wrong. I would later come to respect Rocky Mountain bighorns as the hardest North American sheep to kill. The main reason for this is their habitat. It's not that the mountains containing bighorns are any steeper or any more difficult to climb; they aren't. However, bighorn country is generally heavily timbered, allowing animals more opportunities to remain hidden from sight. In contrast, the places Dall and Stone sheep call home are primarily above the timber, making these sheep more visible.

Upon my arrival in Calgary I was greeted by Leo Muench, a friend of Nayda's. Although Leo wouldn't be hunting, he had always wanted to spend time in the mountains and this was his opportunity. With him were Frank and Lea Lamberti. Frank was an accomplished sheep hunter, but it was Lea who would be the hunter on this trip. Like me, she had already taken both Dall and Stone rams and was seeking the third leg of her slam. Leo drove us to the town of Rocky Mountain House, where we all spent the night.

A short drive the next morning brought us to the trail head, where we were met by Nayda and her daughter Desiree. All-terrain vehicles were used to transport us the remaining ten miles to Nayda's camp in the mountains, where wall tents served as shelters. The setting was majestic, with towering peaks on each side of the valley. The valley bottoms were heavily timbered and the spruces and pines extended quite high onto the slopes, especially in the mountain draws. At higher elevations the trees began to thin out, leaving bare rock in some places and grass in other locations.

Some areas were predominantly bald, while timber was a more prevalent feature in other places.

My guide was to be "Hawkeye" Cadrain and, at least initially, we would be hunting from the main camp. Hawkeye was an interesting but appropriate moniker for a man who was blind in one eye. His single good eye was expertly suited for seeing game animals, as he proved time and again. On September 1st, opening day of the sheep season, we began our search for a bighorn ram.

Over the next two days Hawkeye and I made a big circle, glassing all the available country as we went. We didn't see a single ram, but we did spot several groups of ewes. On one occasion, sheep suddenly materialized from a patch of timber on a hillside we had been looking at for hours. Just when we had concluded that there couldn't possibly be anything hidden in the trees, out popped eight lambs and ewes. That was an eye-opener for me. If the rams were timbered-up like this, we were going to have a tough time of it.

Hawkeye and I arrived back at the main camp just at dark on our second full day of hunting. That night a grizzly bear raided the camp's meat cache, raising all kinds of havoc. The bear stole away with the meat, containers and all. The two of us left in the morning for another two-day excursion into a different drainage. This country was very rocky and rugged. Steep rock walls, waterfalls and some very unusual geologic formations punctuated the landscape. In one place the exposed rock had the appearance of a cross section through a stone jelly roll, with layers of concentrically swirled rock replacing cake. We also saw three different mountain goats but no sheep.

As we made camp for the night it began to rain lightly amid a thickening fog. It rained most of the night and by morning the fog was everywhere. Eventually, the misty curtain began to lift, revealing fresh snow on the upper slopes of the nearby mountains. But just as visibility began to improve, conditions deteriorated and the peaks were once again enveloped in mist. We waited most of the day in the vain hope that the weather would get better. When it became apparent that things were getting worse, we decided to head for camp. By the time we arrived just before dark, snow was falling almost down to the river's elevation.

The next morning dawned cold with a couple of inches of snow on the ground in camp. We could only guess at the levels the high country might hold. Everyone was back in camp and nobody had even seen a ram for our collective efforts. It continued to snow for most of the day with visibility remaining poor. This pattern persisted into the night and all of the following day, making everyone grumpy and anxious for better weather so we could resume hunting.

September 7th finally saw a halt in falling snow and better visibility, but six inches of white now blanketed our campsite. Nevertheless, it looked like conditions were good enough to resume hunting. However, nobody expected an easy time of it! Hawkeye and I were headed to a new area, assisted initially by the all-terrain vehicles. As we rode, snow-laden branches transferred their moisture to us as we unavoidably contacted the bent boughs of brush. When the trail ended we continued higher on foot. The farther we climbed, the more ferocious the wind became. By the time we reached a high plateau, we estimated the wind speed to be a steady forty miles per hour, with gusts to sixty. Spruce trees only four feet in height were leaning at a forty-five-degree angle due to the wind's force. At the same time, the temperature was steadily dropping. Despite the horrendous conditions, we did see some lambs and ewes, as well as one very good non-typical mule deer buck just before dark.

The coming night would prove to be the most trying of my sheep-hunting career. Hawkeye chose a campsite in the thickest grove of spruces he could find. Even so, there was a foot of snow on the ground and the wind whipped about with fury. We didn't have a tent, and the tarp which was supposed to provide protection didn't last long. A sleeping pad placed on the snow served as a platform for my sleeping bag. Between the wind and the sub-freezing temperatures, I honestly thought I might freeze to death before the sun returned. Sleeping was impossible, and all night long I did pushups in my bag to stave off the cold.

The wind was still blowing fiercely the next morning, but a cloudless day held the promise of warming temperatures. The two of us headed to a good glassing location, but the wind buffeted us badly, making it difficult to do a thorough job. Around 10am, despite watering eyes, I spotted some movement. When Hawkeye looked through the spotting scope he was able to confirm the presence of seven rams, including at least two shooters. After satisfying ourselves that they were bedded for the day, we began our approach.

In some places the snow was piled into drifts three feet high, but Hawkeye and I steadily closed the distance. Three hours after we had first spotted them, we were positioned above the rams and ready to make our final stalk. As we slowly crept up the ridge searching for a good place to shoot from, all hell broke loose. The first sign of disaster was when we observed a lone ram running down across the flats, some 500 yards below us. A moment later the other rams appeared down the slope, but they followed a different and slightly more favorable route. These sheep weren't moving any slower than the first ram, but instead of tracking farther from us, they were paralleling our position some 300 yards away. As I sat in the snow to stabilize my shooting platform, Hawkeye shouted to take the lead ram.

My first shot missed, but I led the ram by approximately three feet for the second shot and it connected. The ram went down, and Hawkeye began slapping me on the back. Just then, the sheep regained his footing and disappeared along with his comrades! To say the least, we were stunned by the turn of events. We both figured we had pulled off a miracle rescue of a blown stalk. Instead, we apparently had a wounded sheep on our hands, and the prospect of recovering the animal was uncertain at best.

Neither of us knew where—or how hard—the ram had been hit. Once the entire group disappeared from sight, we went down to look for blood evidence which might help us out. Unfortunately, when we arrived at the spot where the sheep had been, we could barely tell that six sheep had passed by only moments before. The wind-driven snow had practically obliterated any evidence of their existence! We were able to track the rams across the open hillside for about two miles, but only by finding spots where the sheep crossed through places protected from the sign-destroying effects of the still brutal wind. The definite but scant blood sign we found also confirmed that the wounded ram was among the larger group. Eventually, though, we were forced to give up the search.

Sick doesn't begin to describe how I felt as it became apparent that the ram would allude us, probably to die later from a bullet I had dispensed. With the advantage of hindsight, it didn't take long for me to appreciate the fact that I had taken a shot that was extremely unwise and foolhardy. The frustration of the previous days and the excitement of the moment had overpowered reason and respect for the animal, leading me to commit a serious lapse in judgment. The wounding of animals always bothered me, but this regrettable episode topped the list. It's one thing to have a branch deflect an otherwise well-placed bullet or to make an uncharacteristically poor trigger pull. Those things occasionally happen to all who hunt. To take a shot where the outcome is determined by sheer luck instead of skill is unforgiveable!

The poor weather and the apparent scarcity of rams had been discouraging. The subsequent blown stalk and especially my "Hail Mary" shot, which had wounded a magnificent animal, destroyed what remained of my mental reserve. Although a few more days were available to hunt, after wounding the ram, all I wanted to do was go home. I'd had enough. Besides, I honestly felt that through my irresponsibility, I had forfeited any legitimate claim I might have had to put my tag on another animal.

When Hawkeye and I arrived back in camp we retold our tale of woe, much to the chagrin of Nayda, who also understood the likely plight of a wounded sheep in such an unforgiving environment. On the plus side, Leo was as ready to bail as I was, so we made plans to leave the next morning. As we drove back to Calgary together he said, "Before I came here, I would have paid anything for the opportunity; having been here, you couldn't pay me enough to go back." Although Leo's sentiments weren't an exact match to mine, I was just as eager to put my time in Alberta behind me. And so, my initial foray hunting bighorn sheep came to an end.

It wasn't much of a consolation prize, but for the first time in my limited experience I wouldn't have to worry about getting my trophy home. State and Provincial game authorities normally require successful hunters to have their horns checked. While these agencies have a bona fide interest in collecting harvest data so they can manage their game populations wisely, as well as ensure that animals have been taken in compliance with the law, these visits are often cumbersome and time consuming. Even after the all the measurements have been logged and the relevant paperwork completed, the challenge of transporting the cape and horns remains.

If at all possible, I always prefer to take these priceless items with me on my flights home. This often requires some ingenuity. Ideally, the airlines are lenient enough to allow the horns onto the planes in my carry-on bag, so I can store them in an overhead bin. That way, they never leave my sight. The viability of this option often depends on which ticket agent is drawn, however. Alternatively, if need be, I place them in my checked baggage, which requires great care to ensure they're protected from careless baggage handlers. The worst-case scenario involves leaving trophies behind and trusting that they'll be adequately protected and promptly shipped to your door. This option has little to recommend it, unless you enjoy additional expense, constant worry and not having your horns available to show off.

Compared to my hunt of the previous year this hunt had been very easy, at least from a physical perspective. However, the mental challenges more than made up for any diminishment in effort needed to traipse around the country. To be sure, all sheep hunts have a substantial mental component, but nothing seemed to go well on this occasion. At every juncture it seemed as though my resolve was being tested. Eventually, it was mental—not bodily—fatigue which made it easier for me to abandon reason and respect for a grand animal, and replace those admirable qualities with my selfish desire to be successful.

The high country of Alberta, Canada. Although the tops of the mountains are bare in many places, timber is always near at hand in bighorn sheep country.

The rocky majesty of Alberta, Canada. Note the diagonal layers of strata which give testament to our planet's violent past.

DALL SHEEP—1993

Subsequent to my bighorn hunt I found myself in somewhat of a quandary. I found sheep hunting to be exciting and challenging and I wanted to continue to enjoy the mountains. However, my latest hunt had been a disappointment, souring an immediate repeat effort towards Grand-Slam® status. For all practical purposes, that left Dall sheep as the likely objective of my next hunt. As a means of interjecting novelty and greater difficulty into my sheep-hunting experience, I entertained the idea of hunting with a muzzle-loading rifle. I had hunted deer in my home state of Massachusetts for many years using a black-powder gun, and I really enjoyed the challenge offered by the primitive weapon.

I decided to use the upcoming FNAWS convention to search for an outfitter who would be willing to make his life more difficult than need be, and help me get within muzzle-loader range of a Dall ram. In order to avoid any misunderstandings, I planned to be completely honest about the limitations that accompanied my choice of firearm. Due to the fact that each round must be constructed in real time from individual components of gun powder and bullet, it was unrealistic to expect that more than one shot could be taken at an animal. More importantly, my effective range would be severely reduced in comparison to what could be expected if I was to hunt with a modern center-fire rifle. Excessive bullet drop and my insistence on using iron sights to aim the rifle meant my maximum practical shooting range would only be a bit more than 100 yards.

When I discussed my goals with Alaskan guide/outfitter Ken Fanning, he seemed intrigued with the concept. He felt his hunting area in the Alaska Range would allow us to stalk sheep to within my self-imposed shooting distance. We'd need some luck and we would have to pick our spots, of course, but I had already concluded that my choice of weapon would necessarily limit shooting opportunities. Judging by the pictures at his booth, Ken's hunting grounds held some spectacular scenery. The more I spoke to Ken the more comfortable I became with him, his operation and my chance of success. Before I left the convention for home, I made arrangements for a hunt in mid-August.

I spent the months immediately prior to the hunt hiking with weight in my backpack and making sure I could shoot the muzzleloader to the best of my abilities. My gun was a Thompson/Center Renegade in .54 caliber. My pet load consisted of a 425 grain Hornady Great Plains bullet in front of 90 grains of Goex black powder. Ignition was accomplished via #11 percussion caps. By the time I left for Alaska I was confident I could place my shots in the vital zone of any sheep that allowed me to approach to within 125 yards.

When I arrived in Fairbanks, Ken's wife Jill was there to meet me. After overnighting in a hotel, the plan was to take a charter flight into sheep camp the next day. Unlike many of his colleagues, Ken had made a conscious choice not to become a pilot. Over the years, he had seen too many of his fellow outfitters meet untimely ends while attempting to navigate planes in the marginal flying conditions which were all too frequently found in the mountains.

The flight into camp was notable for two things. First, the single-engine Helio aircraft I was on was cruising about 3,000 feet above the valley floor when an Air Force A-10 Warthog was observed swooping into a side valley of the nearby mountains. As it headed back in our direction, the jet actually passed between us and the ground as our pilot tipped his wings to ensure we were seen. Second, as we dropped over the glacial moraine which bordered the camp, preparatory to landing on a flat stretch of gravel, the wreckage of a less fortunate single-engine plane lay to the side as it awaited spare parts and the repairs which would again make it serviceable. As I later learned, the damage was relatively minor and no one had been injured in the mishap.

The setting for my hunt was quite unusual. We were located on an island of sorts. The central feature was picturesque Mt. Hayes, a major ice and snow-covered peak towering nearly 14,000 feet above sea level. Mountains similar to those I had experienced on my first trip to the Alaska Range dominated the lower elevations. As before, the bald tops consisted primarily of black gravel and shale before giving way to vegetated side slopes as the mountains lost elevation. Instead of being surrounded by water, however, this alpine island was totally enveloped by ice. Mt. Hayes and the two ice-clogged arms of the same-named glacier completed the circle. When viewed from a distance, the vista appeared to have three distinct vertical zones. The verdant green of the middle layer contrasted starkly with the white snow and ice above and below, providing dramatic visual appeal.

Ken welcomed me to the Alaska Range as I disembarked the airplane. His base of operations featured two small but decent buildings constructed from stone, mortar and wood. One of Ken's assistant guides, Lee Baumgart, walked into camp just before supper. He had hiked from another camp some miles away. After a tasty supper of sheep loins we settled down for the night, full of anticipation for what the new day might bring.

The next morning, the three of us took a walk a couple of miles up the glacier to a spot where we could effectively glass for sheep in a side basin. It didn't take long to locate a group of ten rams, but they were bedded in an inaccessible spot. Given their location, the best course of action was to wait for them to move someplace more advantageous. Unfortunately, they stayed put the entire day. While we waited, about 30,000 feet above us, the U.S. Air Force was conducting a major military exercise of some sort. Tanker planes could be seen refueling multiple fighters as they queued for a spot at the jet-fuel spigot.

Finally, around 5pm, the rams stirred and began to feed. Once we determined where they were headed, the three of us began to close the distance. Although it's impossible for sheep to maintain peak alertness while they're moving and eating, we still had ten sets of eyes to contend with. Plus, we didn't have a lot of cover available to hide our movements. Nevertheless, using undulations in the terrain, we were able to get within shooting range. Eventually, four rams appeared fifty yards below us, feeding as they walked. Before we had an opportunity to evaluate them, however, the biggest ram saw us as we attempted to melt into the hill. The entire group quickly reversed course and disappeared around the convexity of the hillside before we could react. They eventually reappeared 200 yards away—well within rifle range—but that didn't help me. Even though I didn't have a chance to shoot, the stalk had been exciting.

Ken, Lee and I looked for and found these same rams, as well as a handful of new ones, on the island the next day. Again, the rams had chosen a bedding location that was unapproachable and when they did move, the change in locations offered us no improvement in prospects. When we didn't immediately locate the rams the following morning, we decided to cross the glacier and hunt the mountains on the other side.

Glaciers are very interesting natural phenomena. Although they may not have an actual heartbeat, they are alive. Glaciers move, expand and contract, melt and freeze, and eerie sounds emanate from them as various forces vie for dominance. Moraine consists of the rocks and soil piled to the sides of a glacier. It's not unusual for the moraine to rise 40-50 feet above the surface of the glacier. A moulin is a vertical hole through the glacial ice which serves as a conduit for running water. Some of these structures are large enough to comfortably house a human, although it would be suicidal to enter without the proper ice-climbing gear and expertise.

The surface of most glaciers is highly irregular, making it almost impossible to traverse one in a straight line. Instead, crossing is more like being in a maze. Huge chunks of ice and/or boulders often teeter on very small footprints, where the slightest of disturbances or a small amount of additional melting could result in the sudden shift of tons of material. Although all glaciers are frozen, a white surface is far from universal. Oftentimes the top layer of ice contains embedded gravel, producing a predominantly brown hue. Whatever the coloration, the footing is routinely marginal unless crampons and ice axes are used to increase traction.

The glacier the three of us had to cross was about a mile wide. It wasn't particularly dangerous; nevertheless, I had to pay very close attention to keep from falling. Once on the other side, we climbed up and over the moraine before ascending to a saddle separating two peaks. From there, we spotted two rams below us and they appeared to be in a favorable location for a stalk. We crept closer, assured ourselves that they were still in position, and then began our final approach.

During the remainder of the climb the rams would be out of our sight, but we expected them to be about 100 yards away when we arrived at our projected shooting location. When we peered over the crest of the ridge, though, the sheep were gone. Unbeknownst to us, the rams had moved higher in the interim. The result was predictable: Instead of us looking down on unsuspecting sheep, they were alerted and glaring down at some very unwelcome visitors. Despite the juxtaposition in elevation and the fact that we had lost the element of surprise, the rams were still well within range of a modern rifle. Of course, that wasn't much of a consolation to me.

By the time the three of us returned to camp a light rain had turned into a downpour. We didn't know it at the time, but the precipitation signaled the onset of a prolonged period of weather which would make hunting impossible. For the next three days rain, low clouds, fog and even some fairly heavy snowfall kept us from seeing the mountain tops. Since there was nothing else to do, we spent the time lounging around camp alternately eating, sleeping or reading. The boredom was palpable, but things could have been worse. At least we were dry, we had plenty of food and we weren't stuck in a small tent. Ken entertained us with some hilarious hunting stories and they helped get us through the monotony. By the time the weather cleared, three inches of snow covered the ground near camp. Undoubtedly, the mountain tops held significantly more of the white stuff.

August 24th brought blue skies and excellent visibility, but everything was covered in snow. We now had a new challenge: find what amounted to a few white specks among a veritable sea of white. And that would prove to be mighty difficult indeed. We decided to start our search on the mountain in back of camp, so we worked our way around the corner, using a contour slightly higher than the glacier. From there, we had Mt. Hayes rising directly in front us, and we could glass the upper reaches of the mountain we occupied, as well as the mountain on the opposite side of the glacier.

The three of us looked high and low for a long time before Ken spotted eleven rams directly across the glacier from us. They must have been there the entire time, but we just hadn't been able to distinguish them from their surroundings. Several of the rams were legal, but since we were located in a fairly conspicuous spot, we had to wait for them to move before we could jump into action. While biding our time, we were able to observe a huge avalanche crash off Mt. Hayes. In fact, it was the loud rumble made by the cascading snow and ice which first caught our attention.

Early in the afternoon, the rams decided to move. They climbed higher before cresting the mountain and disappearing from our sight. Confident we were no longer in danger of being detected by the rams' keen eyesight, the three of us packed our gear and crossed the glacier. Since the sheep had topped the ridge, we figured we had a better chance of finding them on the far side of the mountain. Therefore, rather than climbing to where we had last seen the rams, we moved around the toe of the slope and into the next valley. We were inching our way along the base of the hill, glassing upward as we progressed, when Ken noticed a ram well above us in the rocks.

There was no expectation that the rams would descend towards us, so that meant we had to somehow drag ourselves up the near vertical rock to within shooting range without being seen, heard or scented. And that wasn't going to be easy! Ken saw an opportunity to advance a couple of hundred yards by using a rocky spine for concealment. We were forced to climb single-file, but despite the poor footing we managed to improve our position. Surprisingly, when Ken peeked over the spine's crest his gaze was returned by a whole herd of sheep as they looked down in our direction.

The rams, ewes and lambs had obviously been alerted by the sound of falling rock, occasionally and unavoidably loosened during our ascent. The group of at least twelve animals stood shoulder-to-shoulder and three rows deep as they tried to gauge the threat we posed. One thing was for sure: the moment of truth had arrived. We were pinned down and the sheep were getting nervous. After several seconds, the sheep began to file off, one at a time. A single legal ram lingered for a last look. When he was clear of any other sheep I decided to take the nearly head-on shot.

I was standing in a narrow depression behind the rocky outcropping, looking uphill at a steep sixty-degree angle. The ram was quartering towards me about 125 yards away. Using the available rocks to help support my non-shooting hand and digging in my toes to keep from losing my footing, I carefully aimed and pulled the trigger. The ram dropped a split second later and began tumbling towards us. For a couple of seconds, I honestly thought he might barrel right into the three of us. Since we had no means of escape, we would have been knocked down like so many bowling pins. Fortunately, the ram came to rest on a small bench just above our hiding spot.

After the danger of the falling sheep had passed, excitement began to wash over the three of us, especially me. I had actually taken a Dall ram with an iron-sighted black-powder firearm under difficult circumstances, and the sense of accomplishment was as intense as it was delicious. Ken, Lee and I climbed the few remaining yards to the dead ram, where we had room for handshakes and congratulations for a collective job well done. To be honest, the ram wasn't the biggest one in the larger group, but that hardly mattered. He was the only one I had a chance to shoot, and I couldn't have been prouder! As Ken had said earlier in the hunt, "There's no such thing as a shitty full-curl ram."

It was a beautiful day and there was plenty of daylight left, so we took a ton of pictures before processing the ram for the journey back to camp. As Ken and Lee worked on the ram, I climbed to the top of the ridge in an attempt to satisfy my curiosity regarding the whereabouts of the rest of the sheep, especially the rams. When I looked over the ridge, the other ten rams were milling around on the opposite slope, a scant eighty yards away. With Mt. Hayes as a backdrop, it made for quite a sight!

The bullet had done quite a job smashing up the ram. The near shoulder was broken, followed by the neck as the bullet continued its path upward and backward. The ram had died instantaneously, which was a great relief to me given what had transpired just a year ago. With the sheep finally in pieces we loaded up our packs. Lee carried most of the meat, while I insisted on taking the ram's head, horns and cape. It was a little treacherous getting down off the mountain, mainly due to the steepness, but once we reached the valley the rest of the walk was pretty straightforward. We arrived back at camp around 7pm, tired and smelling like animal parts but completely content from the day's effort.

All in all, this hunt hadn't seemed very difficult. This was mainly due to the fact that rams were in close proximity and we never had to do much climbing. This was in contrast to all my previous hunts, and a reflection of the rather unique setting. It's also true that we lost three days of hunting to the weather, and you don't work very hard when you're cooped up in a hut, even though the mental anguish is considerable. Finally, from an enjoyment perspective, the beauty of Mt. Hayes and its environs finished a close second to that experienced by the taking of my ram. In my estimation, my second trip to the Alaska Range and my first sheep hunt with a muzzleloader had been an unmitigated success.

The vegetated lower slopes in the foreground give way to the snow and ice of 14,000-foot Mt. Hayes in the background.

Mt. Hayes after it snowed. Finding white sheep against a nearly universal white backdrop proved challenging.

My first sheep with a muzzleloader—near Mt. Hayes, Alaska.
Photo by Ken Fanning

Stone Sheep—1994

My decision to use a primitive firearm on my last hunt was a significant milestone in my sheep-hunting career. My willingness to make an already tough task even more difficult demonstrated that I had achieved a level of comfort with the mental and physical rigors posed by the mountains. I expected that my self-imposed limitations would likely force me to hunt longer and harder for opportunities. I also realized that I faced the distinct possibility of going home empty-handed. The fact that I had accepted these risks and I had prevailed despite them was both instructional and encouraging: I now knew that, under the right circumstances, it was possible to get within muzzleloader range of a sheep; my confidence in my own attributes and abilities was cemented; and my desire to continue testing myself was only fueled by the experience. When hunting sheep, as it is with many other facets of life, I had come to appreciate that the sense of reward was commensurate to the difficulty of the endeavor.

At the FNAWS convention in January, I was eager to find a Stone sheep outfitter who hunted an area that might be favorable to me and my smoke pole. I was predisposed to contract with smaller outfits, mainly because I felt they were more likely to provide me with a high level of individual attention during the course of my hunt. For me, it came down to this consideration: I didn't want to be sheep hunter #13 when I could be Paul Carter, our client for the second hunt. Now that my weapon of choice was a muzzleloader, I sought any special accommodations that might aid my hunt, whether they be a specific hunting location within the larger hunting area, the most experienced guide the outfit had to offer or an extra hunting day or two. As always, I was honest about my needs and desires, and I expected no less from prospective outfitters. In the final analysis, any contractual agreement would be a mutual one, based upon the realistic expectations of both parties.

I was very fortunate to find an outfitter who was a good match for me at the convention. Kostynuk Outfitting was a small family-run outfitting business, and they controlled a handful of Stone sheep tags. Started by Sam and his wife Marion, they originally conducted bighorn hunts in Alberta, but they had been operating for the past several years out of northern British Columbia. Their son Calvin had assumed control of most of the field responsibilities, although Marion retained her status as the self-described mouthpiece of the outfit. The Kostynuks seemed like great people and Calvin thought that killing a Stone ram with my muzzleloader was within the realm of the real. With all my concerns satisfactorily addressed, I booked with them for August. Besides Stone sheep, the hunt included mountain goat as a second animal.

Upon my arrival in Smithers I met two other hunters—Richard Mussleman and his friend Van Probst. Van's wife Kay was along to help film his hunt. If he took a Stone sheep, Van would achieve Grand-Slam® status in four hunts over just four years, and he would have accomplished the feat on the cheap! He had drawn a desert bighorn tag in his home state of California on the first try and a Rocky Mountain bighorn permit in Wyoming the following year. A reduced-price cancellation hunt for Dall sheep followed, and a similarly fortuitous break had landed him in British Columbia. He's still the luckiest man I've ever met.

We were all scheduled to fly into the Kostynuk's main camp at Cake Lake via a DeHavilland Beaver float plane, my first time on floats. Kay and I both got sick during the flight despite taking Compazine before boarding. At least I had someone to share the misery with this time. Upon landing, I met my guide Roy Milner and the rest of the Kostynuk's crew. I also learned that horses were used to make the large guiding concession a little easier to navigate. Once we reached one of the many outlying spike camps, however, most of the hunting would be on foot in traditional backpack style. That pleased me, as I was no expert horseman.

Hunters spend a lot of time evaluating outfitters before selecting someone to take them on a guided hunt. Outfitters do the same with prospective clients, especially when the hunting can be expected to be strenuous. Although everyone's money is green, it's not in the outfitter's best interest to put clients in situations they are not prepared for or where the chance of success is non-existent. Thus, outfitters constantly assess their hunters for experience and fitness in an attempt to match abilities to the hunting environment. While lounging around Cake Lake, Calvin reminded me of this fact via an innocuous comment he made regarding equipment. He stated that it was reassuring to have a hunter show up with an obviously well-worn backpack held together with Duck Tape® and baling wire; a hunter who came to camp with a shiny new pack was viewed with suspicion.

Everyone left the lake the next day. Roy, Calvin and I headed to Shovel Camp. Aided by a well-worn trail, the trip only took a couple of hours. The camp was situated in a beautiful high-alpine meadow with gorgeous mountains all around. After unpacking the horses and setting up camp, we ate a good supper and called it a day. The real hunting was to commence in the morning.

The three of us rode to a high saddle the next day, gaining a lot of elevation in the process. After Roy and I assembled our gear, Calvin took the horses back to Shovel camp. We would hunt the neighboring country for a couple of days and Calvin would return to extract us at a predetermined time. High on the mountain, the first thing I noticed was how hazy it was. Forest fires far to the north were spewing enough smoke that our visibility left something to be desired, especially given the cloudless day. Roy and I walked a couple of miles before setting up camp in a protected spot a couple of hundred feet below the mountain's crest.

With all the preliminaries finally behind us, it was time to start hunting in earnest. Roy and I only had about half a day available to us, but the remaining hours turned out to be packed with action. First, we hadn't traveled far from the tent when we encountered a lone young ram while traversing a shale ledge. We stopped in our tracks upon seeing the ram, but the youngster just kept inching closer even though we were completely in the open. Unbelievably, the ram eventually bedded at eye level in the rocks, a scant five yards away! I guess he liked our company.

Later in the day, as the two of us were about to turn the corner to enter some heretofore unexplored piece of real estate, I happened to look back over my shoulder. Standing on a distant tall pinnacle was a mature ram. We instantly reversed course and secured a favorable vantage point some 400 yards above the ram. Closer observation revealed five rams in all, including two definite shooters. The rams were in a perfect place for our stalk, but one problem remained: a single hour of daylight was all the time available to us. Even if we didn't pursue the sheep, we'd need every minute to make it back to the tent. Rather than rush the stalk and possibly spook the sheep out of the country, we decided to slink back to our campsite while we still had enough light. After all, the rams were content and we'd surely have no trouble finding them first thing in the morning.

Sleep came hard that night as I couldn't help but anticipate how things would play out the next day. Before long the new day dawned and Roy and I quickly headed back to the previous day's lookout. However, there wasn't a sheep to be found! We glassed every nook and cranny, changed our position slightly and glassed some more—all to no avail. We couldn't believe it, but we weren't giving up. Figuring the rams had to be on the mountain somewhere, we decided to do some serious looking. We circled the entire peak twice that day, once fairly high and another time closer to the base. For all our glassing and walking, we didn't see a single sheep anywhere, and we were at a complete loss as to where the rams might have gone. The whole episode was both unbelievable and unexplainable!

Our frustration was only compounded by the seventy-degree temperatures and by the thickening smoke, which was increasingly handicapping our ability to see long distances. Besides that problem, the accompanying acrid smell wasn't particularly enjoyable, either. To make matters worse, on one of our traverses of the mountain I was able to evaluate our set-up from the previous evening, and I discovered that we could have enjoyed an eighty-yard shot had we only had the benefit of just a little more daylight. That sad realization put an exclamation point on an utterly discouraging day.

Roy and I hunted the same mountain again the following day, but we still couldn't locate the band of five rams. However, we did inadvertently spook a different bachelor group of three rams. They were bedded below us in the rocks as we climbed, and we never saw them until they bolted. The rams stopped briefly about 200 yards away before they resumed their sprint to another mountain. Later in the day, fully disgusted by our lack of luck, we retrieved our tent and headed back to the saddle to meet Calvin. He was waiting for us, and we all descended to Shovel camp. Our three-day excursion, which had begun with such promise, ended with a thud.

The three of us packed up camp the next morning and rode almost five hours to another campsite. Without the horses, accessing this much real estate would have been impossible. But dealing with horses had several disadvantages: they required time and attention; they had to be be rounded up and saddled before anyone could go anywhere; and they had to be fed, shod and cared for. By the time we arrived at the new camp, most of the day was shot. Calvin was able to radio Sam at the lake, discovering that Van and Richard had both taken sheep already. Although I was happy for them, I didn't relish my role as the only hunter who hadn't connected. On the positive front, Roy and I had put a lot of miles behind us over the previous days, and my feet had paid a price. A day without any climbing or sidehilling provided some welcome relief.

Roy and I spent the next couple of days searching the nearby hills for rams. Sheep and other game were quite plentiful. All told, we found a bull moose, fifteen goats and eleven different Stone rams. Most of the rams weren't legal, but one band of six sheep held two shooters. They weren't real big, but I wasn't picky. When the rams left their beds we attempted to get closer. We figured we'd find them feeding leisurely in the vicinity of their bedding area, but despite the fact that the wind had been perfect and we had good cover, the rams had completely vacated the premises. Besides being unsuccessful, our stalk had been conducted in the face of a particularly nasty driving snow and ice storm, which only added to our discomfort.

The highlight of those days was the scenery. The wind direction had changed, taking the smoke with it. This brought the majesty of the mountains into better focus and made for improved photographic opportunities. Although every view held beauty, one scene stood out. Roy and I were positioned on a ridgeline where we could look across the valley at another mountain which contained five peaks. Spilling from the low point between each peak were pastel-colored rocks. Remarkably, each saddle contained a different color—green, blue, orange and tan. It appeared as though some unseen force on the far side of the mountain was pouring vast quantities of paint through the gaps, just for our exclusive enjoyment.

The next day, August 23rd, was as grueling as it was frustrating! Roy and I walked from camp to the head of the valley, and then over the ridge to another drainage. Just as we topped the ridge the wind really picked up, followed in short order by horizontal snow. As we huddled behind an outcropping of rock to minimize our exposure to the elements, Roy spotted some sheep feeding across the valley in a grassy section of the next mountain. Three of the five sheep were rams, but the blowing snow prevented a more detailed evaluation. Roy figured at least one of the rams would be legal, although he had no way of knowing for sure. Under different circumstances, we might have remained where we were and waited for a better look through the spotting scope. Given the weather, staying put didn't seem very attractive, so we decided to try to get closer to the rams.

The two of us descended before starting up the opposite slope. As we approached the grassy area, we noticed two rams casually walking along the edge of the timber 300 yards in front of us. When they disappeared from sight we continued to cautiously advance until we cleared the last few remaining spruces, giving us an unobstructed look at the area where the sheep had been feeding. Instead of finding sheep standing in the open as we had expected, the hillside was devoid of wildlife! We had been given the slip once again. We eventually observed the ewe and her lamb well above us, but the three rams were nowhere to be found.

Roy and I didn't know it at the time, but Calvin had been glassing the same area from a peak closer to camp. He saw two rams (he might have missed the third) descend, cross a small creek and climb a mountain to our left. Armed with that piece of the puzzle, we concluded that the rams had gone down the slope just as we were going up, and we had crossed paths in the timber. All this was interesting, but Roy and I had added another fifteen miles to our pedometers, and we had nothing to show for the effort.

We started back up the valley the next morning, this time on horses, intent on finding the rams which had eluded us the previous day. Halfway to the valley's end, however, we noticed two rams on the mountain to our right. When they bedded in a favorable spot we decided to give them a try. Our stalk put us within range above them, but just as we were setting up the shot a nearby marmot started whistling. The rams became nervous and within seconds they walked out of our sight, even though they hadn't actually detected our presence. I couldn't help thinking: that if it weren't for bad luck, we'd have no luck at all.

At the start of every hunt, Father Time pulls out an hourglass, turns it end for end and grains of sand begin dropping from the full side to the empty side. Naturally, the hourglass only holds a finite number of sand particles, which continue to fall at an even rate of speed. To the hunter, though, each successive sunset brings with it a feeling that the passage of time is accelerating. When the hunt begins it seems as though the available time is limitless; by the hunt's mid-point, there's a conspicuous sense that the hunt is inexorably slipping away.

Like it or not, my hunt was winding down, and the pressure to put a sheep on the ground was mounting, not just for me but for Roy also. I had come to British Columbia with high hopes of shooting two animals. I would have gladly settled for a single Stone ram. The way things were going, it was becoming increasingly likely that I wouldn't even get to pull the trigger. At some point, in my bedeviled state of mind, I said as much to Roy. Without hesitation he replied, "You're going home with both animals."

Early on August 25th, we started our ride up the valley. This time, no rams were there to tease us away from our prime objective: another go at the three rams which had disappeared on us two days earlier. Roy and I left the horses in the trees on the near side of the hill at the valley's head, and began our climb. After clearing that relatively low obstacle, we worked our way to the left of the creek and started up the more formidable mountain where the rams had sought refuge the last time we had entered this theater. We hadn't been climbing very long when Roy spotted the rams well above us on the slope.

The sheep eventually settled down and we carefully used the available cover to close the distance to about 350 yards. But that was as far as we could go. Unless the rams moved we were stuck right where we were. Not unexpectedly, the two of us spent the next eight hours staked to our hiding place, as the rams luxuriated in the full sunshine and pleasant temperatures. Waiting all those hours definitely wasn't easy, but at least we weren't being pelted by blowing snow and ice, as we had been on previous occasions. At long last, the rams started feeding around 6pm.

Unfortunately, the rams headed deeper into the basin and away from us. Leaving most of our gear behind, Roy and I used the opportunity to creep closer, eventually cutting the distance to 200 yards. Of course, this game of hide and seek was time-consuming, and the sun was continuing its race to the horizon. But just when it looked as though our efforts might be for naught, something completely unexpected occurred: A group of lambs and ewes appeared from beyond the rams, feeding towards us. And that caused the boys to reverse direction.

The remaining problem was one of time and position. This high on the mountain, Roy and I didn't have much vegetation to hide behind, so we couldn't just run all over the place and expect that we wouldn't be seen. Instead, we had to guess where on the slope the rams might come back through, get ourselves to a suitable ambush point without being detected, and pray that our position would be within muzzleloader range. If the rams crossed too far above or too far below us, I'd have no shot. Besides that, we had no control over when the sheep might pop into the shooting corridor, if at all. If the rams took their time, they could run out the clock on the day's hunt, as the rapidly fading daylight would soon prevent me from seeing my gun's sights. We'd need some luck to be sure, but so far, good fortune was the hunt's most conspicuously absent ingredient.

Recognizing that one moving person was more likely to escape detection than two, Roy and I decided I should advance alone. When the sheep briefly disappeared from view, I quickly moved up the mountain so I could cover the most likely travel routes. All I had for cover was a patch of pucker brush which was no more than a couple of feet high. After what seemed like an eternity, around 8pm, a single ram walked into view about 125 yards up the hill. My preference was to wait for a better opportunity, but the wind was iffy. I realized that, if I was going to kill a sheep, the time had come.

This wasn't going to be an easy shot, as it would be taken from an unsupported sitting position and at the extreme limit of my effective range. I steadied myself as best I could and touched the trigger. The shot missed completely, but rather than bolting, the ram just climbed a little higher. I had a speed-loader in my pocket, giving me one last chance to salvage the day and the hunt. Flattening myself behind the brush, I managed to push powder and bullet down the barrel using my ramrod. After putting a new percussion cap on the nipple, I slowly sat back up and found the ram standing broadside. He was farther away than before, but not significantly so.

Oddly, my sights seemed steadier for my second shot than they had been for the first. After the gun belched this time, a distinctive "whack" echoed back to me. I assumed this was the sound of bullet hitting flesh. However, the ram reacted by taking a couple of short jumps and then he resumed walking. My heart sank as my mind registered the bitter prospect of failure. But before any permanent heartbreak could grip me, the ram fell over!

Two hundred yards below, Roy stood and we silently acknowledged our good fortune. He signaled that he would go down to retrieve our packs, and I started my climb up to the fallen ram. Frankly, I needed the time alone. To this point, I had barely been able to keep the growing sense of discouragement in check as the travails of the past two weeks fought, day after day, to erode my resolve. The ups and downs of the last few minutes had added even more tumult to an already overworked psyche. With the ram's death all those burdens were instantaneously removed, releasing a completely unanticipated flood of emotions. I was grateful that I had been granted the life of a magnificent animal and sad for its demise, proud that I had endured the many hardships and persevered, relieved that the long ordeal was over and content with the outcome. If vitality is measured not by the strength of a beating heart but by the intensity of one's feelings, I could never be more alive than I was at that moment.

As I sat next to the ram and my sub-conscious evaluated the entirety of my experience, tears rolled down my cheeks. I realized that my wet eyes were simply a physical manifestation of my state of mind. I felt no shame, nor did I feel any urgency to hold the tears back. High on the ridge with the sun hanging on the horizon, the purity and honesty of my feelings seemed perfectly matched to the un-embellished natural beauty of the setting that engulfed me. So, I just accepted the moment for what it was.

Roy arrived in short order, and we shared a congratulatory handshake as we admired our trophy together. The ram had a white face, and although he was fairly light in color, his coat took on a darker hue behind his front legs. His horns were quite respectable, especially for this area. Here, extreme cold dominated the winters and the feed wasn't as good as that found in some other parts of British Columbia, so horn growth tended to suffer. What really stood out, though, was the ram's body. He was huge! The head and horns, although normal in size and configuration, seemed disproportionately small when viewed against the rest of the sheep's body.

Unfortunately, time was of the essence, so we hurriedly took pictures and began cutting up the sheep. My preference was to cape the ram for a full-body mount, but given the impending darkness, that would have been too time-consuming. Therefore, I settled for a shoulder mount. My second shot had hit the facing shoulder and passed through both lungs before exiting. We finished our work as the last glimmer of light faded from the sky, and quickly loaded our packs for the downhill walk to the horses. As was fast becoming my custom, I carried the head, horns and cape. By the time we found the horses, it was slightly past 10pm. The ride back to camp was as peaceful and serene as could be imagined, and we arrived around midnight. After sharing our adventure with Calvin and consuming a well-deserved, if belated, supper, we all went to sleep.

Roy and I were in no hurry—and in no condition—to jump right into hunting goats the next morning, so we started the day at a leisurely pace. With a dead ram in camp, we all had jobs to do. Cleaning my gun was at the top of my list. However, before noon the two of us were once again in the saddle for a short ride down the valley. We found a spot where we could glass the appropriately named Castle Mountain. Around 4:30pm, we spied a single goat in an advantageous location, fairly low on the mountain.

Summoning our still-aching muscles for one more climb, we moved up through the trees, brush and shin tangle to within fifty yards of the goat. Roy took one last look through his binoculars, in order to confirm that the animal was a billy, before giving me the thumbs-up sign. My shot took the goat off his feet and he rolled to a stop a few yards down the hill. In less than twenty-four hours we had taken two great trophies, and Roy's earlier prediction about me leaving with both animals had been fulfilled.

My quartering-away shot had resulted in massive internal damage, including the guts, lungs and a broken far-side shoulder. I was able to recover the slug just beneath the skin where it had exited the shoulder. Upon close examination it was apparent that we had done this animal a favor. The goat's front teeth were either severely worn or missing, and he wasn't likely to survive another winter. He was later aged at thirteen years old. We caped the billy for a full mount, then headed down to the horses. We arrived back in camp at 9:30pm, concluding an eventful and productive two-day period.

With all our objectives accomplished, Calvin, Roy and I packed everything the next morning and started down to Cake Lake. Six hours later we joined all the others, setting off an extended round of congratulations and some serious story-telling. The float plane arrived two days later for our return trip to civilization. After a final round of goodbyes, the visiting foursome was in the air to Smithers.

Before leaving for home I had two chores to accomplish. First, our animals had to be brought to the authorities for the compulsory inspections. That was easily accomplished. However, because I had taken the goat only recently, the hide wasn't quite ready for travel. It needed one more application of salt to withdraw the remaining moisture, in order to prevent the hair from slipping. Calvin had given me extra salt, but I wasn't in the wilderness any more. My hotel room would have to suffice for this messy task. The bathtub proved to be a suitable place to re-salt the skin, but the final step in the process required that I dry the hide. How was I going to do that?

I finally decided to hang the goat skin out my second-story window, so the sun and wind could work their magic. I hoped that no one would notice or object. Since I didn't hear from the management, I felt I had succeeded. However, upon removing the newly dried pelt, I was horrified to find the side of the building covered by a white sheen of dried salt. Fearing that I'd later be expected to pay for the building's re-painting, I quickly employed a pail and repeatedly rinsed the salty evidence from the siding. Although I was anxious about the affair at the time, in retrospect, I bet my episode placed fairly low on the list of hunter-based insults the establishment had endured over the years.

My trip to British Columbia had been a triumph of will. Roy and I had succeeded in the face of constant adversity. Like most sheep hunts, we had been hot, cold, wet, sore, sweaty and sunburned. We had endured uncertainty, dread, aggravation and disappointment, almost without limit and well beyond what's considered normal. Without Roy's knowledge, sense of humor, patience and encouragement I would have surely failed to meet the challenge. But in the end, we had prevailed and the sense of accomplishment could only be described as exhilarating and intoxicating.

One of the many eye-catching views from the Kostynuk's hunting concession.

Some more of the gorgeous mountain scenery in northern British Columbia.

The sun's about to set on me and this hard-earned Stone ram, taken with my blackpowder gun.

Photo by Roy Milner

Stone sheep and mountain goat horns taken by three fortunate hunters, posed on a bench outside the Kostynuk's main camp at Cake Lake.

ROCKY MOUNTAIN BIGHORN SHEEP— 1995

With the success of my latest Stone sheep hunt I actually had two separate Grand Slams® half way to completion—one with a rifle and one using my muzzleloader. Nevertheless, I still felt no urgency to pursue either, as the prices for bighorn and desert bighorn hunts continued to be at a premium. By and large, the reason for this disparity could be attributed to the law of supply and demand.

Both of the bighorn species were found in stable numbers in the continental United States, but sheep hunting was strictly controlled through the use of state-issued permits. Prospective hunters were forced to participate in a lottery system of one sort or another, and the odds of drawing a tag were generally prohibitive. It was (and still is) quite common for someone to apply for decades before being drawn, if at all. If you were lucky enough to have your name pulled, though, the cost of the hunt would be reasonable.

Bighorns also existed in parts of British Columbia and Alberta, and desert bighorn sheep were found in portions of Mexico. In contrast to the U.S., hunts in these locations could be booked directly with outfitters, without first securing the permit. However, due to large outfitting areas, relatively small overall numbers of sheep or a combination of the two, the available hunting opportunities were always exceeded by the number of hunters vying for a place at the sheep-hunting table. As a consequence, hunt prices for these two species, whether in Canada or Mexico, were quite high.

I had been applying for coveted sheep tags in the United States for several years. As I evaluated my hunting options for 1995, I wasn't ready to pony up the dollars it would take to hunt the more expensive sheep. At the same time, I thought about expanding my primitive-firearm experiences to other species. So, I booked a brown bear hunt on the Alaskan Peninsula in the fall with old friend Rocky Keen.

In early May, I received the shock of my life. Myron Wakkuri, an outfitter in Wyoming, called to inform me that I had drawn a Rocky Mountain bighorn tag in his home state. My wife and I had befriended Myron and his wife Karma several years prior. Karma had hunted Stone sheep with Art and Crystal Thompson, and I had sought her input before deciding to hunt with Gundahoo River Outfitters. Since then, the four of us had gotten together at the FNAWS conventions, and Janet and I had even taken our kids to the Wakkuri's home in Wheatland as part of a larger tour of Wyoming. Myron and Karma were great people, as was their son Mike, and I was only too happy to put Elk Mountain Outfitters in charge of my bighorn hunt scheduled for September.

I spent the rest of the summer preparing for my wholly unanticipated hunt in Wyoming. I had procured a tag in area #3, which was situated west of Cody, east of Yellowstone Park and south of the highway which connected the two. I was familiar with the locale from our previous visit to the state. In fact, the Carter family had used this very highway to access the Park entrance. My hunt would actually begin at the trailhead known as Elk's Fork, a dozen miles west of Cody, along this same road.

The unexpected bighorn tag presented me with an interesting choice: Should I hunt with a modern rifle or a firearm more commonly at home in the mid-nineteenth century? For me, it wasn't even a close call. I was eager to take the muzzleloader and nothing I heard from Myron discouraged me from doing so. Apparently, getting within 125 yards of a ram was possible in the terrain where I was headed. Besides, at that point in time, to the best of my knowledge, no one had yet taken a Grand Slam® of sheep with a primitive weapon.

On September 16th I left for Wyoming. Karma picked me up at the Laramie airport and drove me to the house in Wheatland. Two days later, with horse trailer in tow, Mike Wakkuri and I started the long drive to Cody. Accompanying us was Tom Herman, who would serve as horse wrangler and camp hand. We stopped briefly in Cody for lunch and some last-minute supplies, before driving the remaining few miles to the trailhead. There, the horses were packed for the lengthy trip up the mountain.

The three of us were headed into the Washakie Wilderness area, to a spot Mike knew well, right in the middle of sheep country. This area was part of the greater Yellowstone ecosystem, and grizzly bears were a serious concern. Extra measures had to be taken to make food stores inaccessible to the omnivores and a can of pepper spray never left Mike's side. The obvious fear that Mike and Tom had for the bears caught me a little by surprise, but I had no doubt their reaction was rational. I had been in grizzly country before, but apparently, the bears around Yellowstone were particularly troublesome.

The hunt didn't get off to a very good start. The ride up the mountain was characterized by increasingly bad weather and almost constant problems with the horses, transforming an expected multi-hour trip into a multi-day slog. Somehow, packs continually loosened from the horses, causing repeated delays. Mercifully, we finally reached our campsite just at dark on the second day of riding. The only positive garnered from the two-day excursion was the knowledge that we hadn't lost any hunting days. Rain and low clouds severely hampered visibility, precluding any search for sheep.

When we woke on the morning of September 20th, two inches of fresh snow coated the ground and visibility was reduced to 100 yards. Hunting sheep was out of the question, so Mike, Tom and I confined ourselves to improving the camp by cutting extra firewood and such. I provided the excitement for the day by inadvertently running the handsaw across the back of my shooting hand. If I had been almost anywhere else, my carelessness would have warranted a trip to the local emergency room for at least five stitches. But we didn't have a hospital close by, nor did we possess sterile sutures. I cleansed the wound as best I could, closed the edges with some self-made butterfly strips and hoped the laceration wouldn't become infected. For some reason, Mike wouldn't let me cut any more wood.

The next day dawned clear but awfully cold for September, approximately ten degrees Fahrenheit. To reinforce the sense that winter had arrived prematurely, a total of six inches of snow now covered the ground at camp, with greater depths expected at higher elevations. Up to this point, there hadn't been much to admire scenery-wise, but the clear blue skies allowed us to enjoy some magnificent snowy vistas.

The day's hunt was long but productive. In all, Mike and I spotted twelve rams in three separate groups during our travels, which encompassed at least ten miles on foot. In one place we accidently bumped a couple of rams, one of which was a real dandy. Unfortunately, they had the drop on us and relocated to an unapproachable section of craggy cliffs. At day's end, I realized that the full sunshine combined with the highly reflective snow and the 10,000-foot elevation had caused my face to become severely sunburned.

The skin on my nose was so badly affected that it became encrusted with a bloody scab that stayed with me for the rest of the hunt.

This was definitely bighorn habitat. With the exception of the highest elevations, timber existed almost everywhere you looked. Of course, uniform blocks of softwood trees weren't the norm. Rather, rocky outcroppings and bald domes were interspersed with the timber, making for a dynamic and varied milieu of feed, escape cover and bedding grounds. As I surveyed the environs, despite the common features of timber and rock, noticeable variations existed from one place to the next. For instance, one mountain consisted mainly of a series of vertical rock pinnacles, while the next peak had a much less severe, rounded profile. There was even a high grassy plain which was chock full of huge boulders. In places, vertical faces of rock formed a fence at the extreme limit of what could be seen.

The country was also enormous in scope. From camp, we could hike for miles in any direction over the undulating terrain and still hunt sheep. Wherever I looked, I couldn't help but be awed by the natural beauty and grandeur surrounding us. Of all the places I've hunted, this patch of Wyoming was as geographically varied and visually interesting as any setting I have been fortunate to experience.

Over the next couple of days the temperature moderated, making for more comfortable hunting and receding snow depths. Mike and I explored the available habitat by eye and by foot, hunting hard each day. We saw some sheep and elk, but nothing noteworthy came of our efforts. Late on the second day, while glassing from the ridge above camp, Mike found a real good ram across the valley. We didn't have enough daylight to immediately exploit his discovery, but we did have every expectation that the ram would be in the same general area the next morning.

September 24th would prove to be an eventful day! As we had anticipated, Mike quickly found the ram not far from where we had seen him the previous evening. Once the ram settled down for the day we mapped out our stalk. The ram wasn't even on the same mountain we occupied, forcing us to give up significant elevation and cross a densely timbered ravine before we could begin the arduous climb back up to the ram's location. This effort would take hours, and the ram would be out of our sight the entire time. Mike left Tom at the glassing location in the hope that he could keep close tabs on the ram, and if necessary, help guide us to him using hand signals once we reappeared on the ram's side of the mountain.

Unbelievably, as Mike and I neared the low point of our descent, we stumbled upon a bedded ram in the thick black timber along the edge of the ravine. This was a different sheep than the one we were after, and he was holed up in a place where no sane sheep hunter would ever expect to find a ram. An elk might seek refuge in such a spot, but sheep liked to use their eyes to detect danger and it was impossible to see far in any direction from this tangle.

Caught completely by surprise, I scrambled to find an opening in the trees as the ram climbed across a rockslide on the opposite side of the gorge. I didn't even have time to slip out of my backpack. I finally found a place to shoot from, sat down and took aim at the ram, which was now walking near the top of the bank some 150 yards away. At the shot, Mike saw the bullet hit the rocks just in front of the ram. A moment later the ram was gone, headed to God knows where. Everything happened so suddenly that it was almost as if the entire episode hadn't taken place. Mike and I were completely flabbergasted at what had transpired, but another ram awaited us and we quickly refocused on our original game plan.

From our present location, we had many hundreds of feet of climbing waiting for us before we'd be anywhere close to our original objective. Somewhere along the way, we encountered a pine tree that was at least three feet in diameter. At this high elevation, a tree that big had to be absolutely ancient! We finally completed our circuitous uphill march, arriving at the base of some steep walls high on the mountain. Confident that the ram had to be somewhere below us on the slope, we rested for lunch.

As the two of us were eating, I happened to glimpse a small ram cross through an opening in the trees a couple of hundred yards below. When I picked up Mike's binoculars to get a better look, the big ram popped into my field of view. We now enjoyed two crucial advantages over the ram: we held the high ground and we knew with certainty where the ram was located. All that remained was to sneak within range, and given the broken nature of the terrain, our chances looked pretty good.

From above, Mike and I carefully advanced parallel to the path the sheep had taken, glassing below us for any sign of the rams. It wasn't long before we found them bedded in a patch of dirt about 130 yards down the slope. The available vegetation and the lay of the land allowed for a closer approach, and I wanted to shrink the shot distance by every yard I conceivably could. Mike suggested I advance alone, so I shed all non-essentials and began to slowly pick my way lower. By creeping and crawling behind the scant cover, I finally closed the range to ninety yards. I had the option of progressing further, but I felt the risk of being detected was too great.

Having made the decision to shoot from my present position, I only needed to sit up without being noticed and assume a stable shooting stance. As I brought the gun to bear, I thought about doing something to roust the ram to his feet, but dismissed that idea as too chancy. I silently cocked the gun's hammer, carefully centered the front bead on the ram's chest and slowly pulled back on the trigger. The gun roared and when the smoke cleared the big ram was on his feet, looking up towards the two of us. Seconds later he disappeared along with his smaller friend. You could have knocked me over with a feather! The sight picture had been good and I felt like I had executed the perfect trigger pull, but the ram was obviously unhurt. I had somehow blown an entirely makable shot, and I felt absolutely sick about it.

I went back up to Mike and apologized for screwing up, and then we both went down to where the ram had been standing to look for evidence of a bullet hitting its mark. There was no blood to be found, but a couple of tufts of hair floated on the rising air currents. Mike was able to watch the rams as they rapidly ascended the next mountain. Obviously, the ram wasn't injured, leaving me to speculate that my shot had gone a tad high, taking some hair off the top of his back in the process.

I suppose it was some consolation that I hadn't wounded the sheep, but that fact was awfully hard to appreciate at the moment. I had wasted a perfect hard-earned opportunity, and I was sure I had let Mike down in the process. I felt like a complete failure, a sensation that would last for some time. In the subsequent days, weeks, months and years, this episode would continue to haunt me as I constantly replayed the series of events in my mind. I still feel like I executed a good shot, but I've always regretted the fact that I didn't wait for the ram to stand. If I had shown more patience, I would have had a significantly larger target at which to aim, and the outcome would have likely begotten joy instead of recrimination.

Mike, Tom and I moved our camp down the valley the next day so we could explore some new country. We still had three days of hunting left before we'd have to leave. We saw sheep each of the next two days, but we just couldn't make anything work, despite all our hard work. The highlight of those days was the rugged beauty of the surrounding mountains. We may not have had an opportunity to kill a sheep, but I was able to capture many wonderful mountain scenes on camera.

September 28th was the last day of the hunt. Mike and I took the horses to an elevated spot on the east side of the valley so we could glass. From there, Mike noticed three rams at the very top of the westernmost mountain. They were so far away I doubted they could even be reached in one day, despite the fact that we had discovered them by mid-morning. In spite of my reservations, which were probably influenced by my dejected state of mind, we decided to give the rams our best effort.

We quickly descended to camp and gave Tom instructions to move the tent further down the valley to where we would be leaving our horses. Then, Mike and I rode lower for the next hour and one-half before tethering the horses. The rest of the hunt would be on foot, and even though we had closed the gap significantly, the rams were still quite distant. We could no longer see the rams, so our only option was to head for their last-known location and hope we'd find them nearby.

After four grueling hours of roundabout climbing, we finally reached the top and looked down into the wooded draw where we had last seen the rams, some seven hours earlier. Mike and I were both beyond parched, as we had long since consumed the contents of our water bottles and our travels had bypassed any additional natural sources of water. Not surprisingly, the rams were gone. However, we could see tracks in the gravel, leading up and out of the draw.

As Mike and I slowly advanced along the ridgeline in the direction the sheep had taken, we could see the highway to Yellowstone Park far below us to our right. About 300 yards into our blind stalk, we observed a good ram about 175 yards away, at a steep uphill angle. Mike thought we could get closer since the ram was feeding with its head facing the hill, completely oblivious to our presence. I narrowed the distance to 150 yards, but one of the heretofore unseen rams spotted me, causing all three sheep to make a hasty exit. Our maximum-effort run at the rams had come up empty. I honestly think that had we arrived just ten minutes earlier, things would have turned out differently.

The sad realization that my hunt was over gripped me as the two of us descended. I was dehydrated, but the only moisture we found on the way down was a crack in a ledge that yielded a few drops of water. We finally limped into camp well after sunset, completely beat from the exhausting day. Tom was there with food and drink to replenish our empty tanks. Early the next morning, the three of us packed up camp and started our long journey back to Wheatland.

As I left Wyoming I couldn't have been more disappointed. I now had two bighorn hunts under my belt, both of which had been unsuccessful. It's one thing to come home empty-handed; that's part of hunting. Bad luck, lousy weather and the like can happen to anyone. However, it's much more difficult to accept failure which can be attributed to deficiencies of performance. In the first instance, a serious error in judgment had cast a pall over my hunt; in the second, my shooting abilities were found wanting. Insofar as it pertained to hunting sheep, after my experience in Wyoming, I honestly didn't know what the future held for me.

The sun peeks through the clouds onto a series of ragged pinnacles in the high country of the Washakie Wilderness.

Sheer walls of stone at almost 11,000 feet.

More Wyoming bighorn country. Notice the timber extending well up the mountain.

A castle-like outcropping of rock high in the wilderness of Wyoming.

DALL SHEEP—1996

As the sour taste left by my latest bighorn hunt began to subside, I eventually came to the realization that I still had the sheep-hunting bug, but I had no specific goal that I was intent on pursuing. It seemed as though every time I became ambivalent about my hunting objectives, I sought refuge from the confusion by returning to Alaska to hunt Dall sheep. And so it would be for 1996. The last time I had hunted the state, I introduced my muzzleloader to the mix as a way of freshening the experience. This time, as a means of adding some excitement and newness, I would be able to bring my wife along too.

Actually, my trips were always a source of conflict for me. I absolutely hated the travel, but I viewed it as a necessary price of admission for the greater glory of the mountains. Part of the problem was due to the fact that, almost invariably, I was a party of one and I had no companion to help pass the long hours in airports and on planes. I also loved my wife and I missed her from the moment I left home. Janet couldn't have been more understanding about my need to hunt, but the separation was undoubtedly hard on her, too. Plus, duties I normally attended to either went undone or fell to her during my extended absences.

I don't remember where, but somehow I discovered an Alaskan outfitter with a unique capability. Ultima Thule Lodge, operated by Paul and Donna Claus, hosted sheep hunts in the Wrangell Mountains, but they also catered to tourists. Their base of operations in the Chitina River valley had amenities that were unheard of for such a primitive setting. Non-hunters didn't just sit around soaking up the scenery, either. River rafting, flight-seeing (sight-seeing by small aircraft) and hiking were just some of the activities one could enjoy. By all accounts, the surrounding big-glacier country also held plenty of large Dall rams.

For a reasonable premium over the hunt cost, Janet could come along and partake in an up-close, real Alaskan experience while I beat myself up in the mountains. Time permitting, once the hunt had concluded we'd have an opportunity to share some of the best that Alaska had to offer. In any event, I would have the benefit of a traveling partner, and I wouldn't have to worry about how things were going back home. Lastly, I had always shared my hunts through the photographs I had taken, and although Janet was impressed by the scenery, I knew that the pictures never quite captured the true majesty of the land. This trip would give Janet the chance to experience the beauty firsthand.

Janet and I began the long journey to Alaska on August 14th. After spending the night in Anchorage, the next morning was devoted to rounding up licenses, powder for my gun and hunting boots. Paul Claus, among other things, was an accomplished mountain climber. Accordingly, he had strong feelings about what constituted proper mountain attire. One of the items he insisted his hunters wear was plastic, double mountaineering boots, which he felt were better suited for his hunting area. I owned a proven pair of leather hunting boots, which I was certain would suffice for the hunt, but I wasn't willing to ruffle any feathers. Still, I wasn't keen on shelling out several hundreds of dollars for a pair of boots I'd probably never use again. Therefore, the alternative was to rent the recommended footwear from an Anchorage sporting goods store.

Once these chores were completed, Ultima Thule employee Johnny Coolidge drove Janet, me and three German tourists to the town of Chitina, where one of the outfit's planes would subsequently fly us into camp. The ride took over five hours but the scenery was grand, especially the Matanuska glacier and the big mountains of Mt. Blackburn, Mt. Drum and Mt. Wrangell seen to the east as we neared our destination. The flight up the Chitina River took less than an hour, and the views were even more impressive. We even saw a grizzly bear fishing in the river. In the vicinity of Ultima Thule's headquarters, the glacier-fed Chitina took the form of a wide braided river.

Upon landing, Janet and I were both flabbergasted by the facilities which awaited us. A two-story log lodge was the central structure, while several log cabins served as auxiliary buildings. Each guest cabin featured running water, flush toilets and showers, as well as comfortable beds and generator-supplied electricity. We were both prepared for more Spartan furnishings, and we couldn't contain our amazement that this level of comfort could be had this far from civilization. It soon became apparent that neither of us would go hungry, as food was both plentiful and delicious. The staff was large, friendly and accommodating.

The next morning my guide, Steve Johnson, and I hunted the mountain behind the lodge. We found seven rams after climbing for half the day. One of the rams was big and we tried to maneuver to within range. Unfortunately, despite the fact that the sheep were in a favorable spot, the wind shifted during our final stalk, spooking the rams and blowing our opportunity to quickly end the hunt. After descending to camp and eating supper, I said my farewells to Janet before Paul flew Steve and me to a new hunting locale in the vicinity of the Hawkins Glacier.

Paul Claus was a legendary bush pilot, and his deft skills were soon apparent as he throttled down the engine preparatory to landing on a glacier at the top of an un-named mountain. The ice wasn't even flat. Instead, the snow field sloped about fifteen degrees from the horizontal. After coming to a smooth but abrupt halt, the plane was emptied, the tail was spun 180 degrees and Paul departed. Steve and I walked a short distance to a more suitable campsite and set up our tent. Never before had I been deposited above the available sheep habitat, where top-down hunting would be the norm, but I relished the prospect. Normally, it was necessary to claw your way up to the sheep.

At Paul's urging, Steve had brought along another guide's rifle—a .280 Remington. Before the hunt I had been assured that my muzzleloader would be appropriate to the setting. Despite those words, my general assessment of the terrain, reinforced by my first day of hunting, caused me to doubt my chances if I insisted on staying exclusively primitive. That sense, combined with the additional knowledge that the area held record-class rams, teased me into accepting the center-fire rifle as an alternative weapon. For the first time since I began hunting sheep with a muzzleloader, I was hedging my bets. I didn't like the feel of that, but it seemed the wise choice.

Steve and I found a band of fifteen rams below us early the following day. It took several hours to get a good look at all of them and determine their trophy status. The group contained two barely legal rams, but given the trophy potential of the area, we felt we could do better. Late in the day we packed our belongings and headed down towards the Hawkins Glacier, where we re-established camp.

By the time the two of us arrived at our new home away from home, I was acutely aware that a compatibility problem existed between me and my rented boots. The outside of both little toes were badly blistered, but a more serious issue centered on the inside of both ankles. Plastic boots incorporate a two-boot system: a soft inner boot fits into a very stiff plastic shell, much like a ski boot. In my particular case, the inner boots incorporated stiffeners along the sides which, for some reason, were digging into my ankles. At this point in time, both ankles were bleeding despite the fact that I had been using mole skin for protection since I first noticed the problem.

Blistered and bruised feet are something every sheep hunter learns to deal with. Downhill walking and traverses across side hills, especially when carrying the added weight of a full backpack, tends to cause foot movement within the boot. Over time, this continual sliding can result in blisters. Socks moist with sweat also facilitate the formation of blisters. If attended to promptly, proper foot care serves to keep things from spiraling out of control.

In this instance, the quandary with my ankles was unusual in regards to its location and it was several magnitudes more serious than any previous difficulty I had encountered. My hunt was in serious jeopardy! You can't hunt sheep if you are unable to walk, and at the moment, I didn't know how much longer I could tolerate the pain. Every step was an effort. Steve and I stopped to attend to my feet as best we could. He even offered to swap boots. I was appreciative, but I believed that the net effect of accepting his proposal would result in both of us becoming crippled.

After doctoring my ankles, we explored the country on the near side of the glacier. Almost immediately, we found a group of five rams. One of the five was an absolute monster—a record-book sheep, for sure! To this day, that ram had the largest set of horns I've ever seen on a living animal. Just the sight of the ram made my feet feel a little better. The rams were moving about, so we tried to get closer. Despite the fact that neither of us felt we had been detected, the rams moved continually higher into the rocks and ice until we were unable to follow. Although we spent the rest of the hunt within sight of the glacier, we never saw that ram again. I guess that's how big old rams get to be that way.

The area Steve and I occupied was nothing less than grand. The mountain peaks were covered in ice and snow, as was the glacier sandwiched between its side moraines. These features reminded me of Mt. Hayes. However, the intermediate ground was as rocky and rugged as any I had encountered in the Chugach Mountains, and it was just as difficult to navigate. The resultant mix of topographies was as imposing as it was picturesque.

Steve and I had seen two decent rams on the far side of the glacier, so we packed up our camp and crossed the river of ice the next morning. The trip took two and one-half hours, and I fell on more than one occasion. By this time, the lay of the land and my suffering feet had convinced me to abandon my black-powder gun in favor of the .280. We climbed up towards the rams, but couldn't find them once we attained elevation. Upon returning to the glacier, we immediately located the rams low on the mountain but working their way higher. Piecing together the evidence, we concluded that they must have come down as we went up; now that we held the low ground, they decided to return to the heights.

Around 5pm, Steve and I made another run at the elusive duo. However, we never closed the gap as they continued to feed higher and eventually disappeared from sight over the top of the mountain, just as the impending darkness forced us to retreat. It had been a frustrating day with a lot of hard climbing thrown in, but at least my ankles seemed to be stabilizing. Our makeshift treatment was apparently keeping the sores from further deterioration.

Steve opened the tent flap at 6am on the morning of August 20th. In the gray light of dawn it wasn't hard to see two white forms feeding above us, moving to our left. We quickly dressed and, when the moment was right, scampered out of the enclosure and up the mountain. It didn't take me long to realize that climbing without the benefit of breakfast, not to mention barely open eyes, was a lot harder than with food in the furnace. Once again, when we arrived at the place where the rams had last been seen, they were nowhere to be found!

Returning to camp, Steve and I backed out onto the glacier in an attempt to locate our ghostly adversaries. Naturally, the rams were still on the mountain, but they were to the right of where they had been previously and they were moving rightward. Somehow, the rams had doubled back without our knowledge, even as we climbed in the rocks with them. Steve and I were really beginning to feel snake-bitten, as these two particular sheep continued to taunt us day after day!

The weather had been perfect, but that night it began to rain and it continued into the following day. For a change, we found three rams across the glacier. Although the monster wasn't among them, at least one of them was good enough to coax us over to that side. Steve and I then ascended towards them through a huge boulder field until we ran out of cover. If we were to have a chance, we'd have to wait them out and hope they moved somewhere more approachable. Fifteen minutes later, for no obvious reason, the rams were running up the mountain. Four hours of hard work were flushed away in an instant.

As the two of us struggled back across the glacier, two rams suddenly appeared on the mountain to our front. Despite our exposed position, the rams hadn't yet noticed our presence. After clearing the moraine we hurried up towards them. Halfway into our climb, I happened to glance down the valley towards the river. What I saw was as eerie and ominous as anything I've ever experienced. A billowing and boiling bank of thick fog was gradually working its way up the main valley floor. As this phenomenon advanced, the visible side valleys were, in turn, inundated by the dark cloud. It didn't take a genius to realize that the murky mess would eventually encapsulate us, ruining the day's hunt in the process.

Steve and I continued our ascent, but the next time I looked down, the glacier couldn't be seen. The mountain tops opposite us were still visible, but they wouldn't be for much longer. We finally made it to the rock outcropping we had chosen as the ambush point for our stalk, but the fog had enveloped us by then and it was getting thicker by the minute. We could hardly see the mountain in front of us, never mind any sheep. Visibility was so poor Steve and I both feared we might not be able to get down safely in the blackening soup, so we decided to abandon our stalk.

Just as we turned to leave, I happened to look up. A temporary hole had opened in the murkiness, and I could identify a sheep standing on a ridgeline some 300 yards away. A quick peek through the binoculars allowed Steve to confirm the presence of a legal ram. I was already getting in position to shoot, and as soon as I received the go-ahead from Steve I pulled the trigger. The ram dropped as if hit by a bolt of lightning, then fell a hundred yards before coming to a stop on a small bench. Seconds later, the window in the gloom slammed shut.

Steve and I were finally thankful for some good luck, but as tempting as it was to climb up to the ram, we still thought the smart play was to go down. Of course, that meant we'd have to come back up tomorrow. We didn't relish that prospect, but neither were we excited about being stranded on the mountain in the dark or incurring an accident as we descended. The ram could wait until conditions improved.

With so much unfinished business, I didn't get much sleep. We were underway early the next morning, and a couple of hours later the two of us approached the scene of the prior night's action. It had rained during the night and fog was still present high on the mountain. As we neared the place where we expected to find our sheep, Steve observed a ram fleeing through the mist, about seventy-five yards away. At the time, we assumed that animal to be the deceased ram's companion, but when we couldn't find a dead sheep, we began to fear the worst.

Steve and I scoured the area searching for clues which might tell us what had happened. Although it had rained, we still found some blood. And, we were able to track the ram's fall by the clumps of hair which had been cut loose by the rocks he slammed into as he tumbled down the mountain. In the final analysis, the objective evidence forced us to conclude that the ram had been wounded, and it had survived both the bullet wound and the precipitous fall. In all probability, we had spooked the injured ram as we entered the immediate area.

Our next task was to perform a broader search and hope we could catch a glimpse of the wounded ram. We explored the area for more than two hours to no avail. Before abandoning our efforts, I decided to return to the place where I had taken the shot, just to put the events in perspective. As I viewed the setting from that angle, I immediately noticed the ram lying on a ledge about 300 yards across the ravine. That particular corner of the hill couldn't be seen from any of our previous vantage points. If I hadn't returned to the spot, I honestly don't believe we would have ever located that ram!

Steve and I now knew where the ram was and it didn't appear he was going anywhere, but one problem remained: we hadn't brought the rifle with us! That sounds incredibly stupid, but we were both positive we had a dead ram on our hands. It was bad enough that we had to climb the mountain an extra time, and we didn't want to carry any more weight than absolutely necessary, especially since we expected to return with a sheep in our packs. Obviously, we figured wrong. While I kept an eye on the ram Steve went back for the gun. Once he returned, it was a simple matter to put the ram out of his misery.

I felt just horrible about the whole affair. Upon examining the trophy, it was evident that my bullet had hit higher than I wanted, clipping the top of the spine. That accounted for the sledge-hammer effect the two of us had witnessed when I fired. The ram had been momentarily paralyzed from the impact, but unbeknownst to us, he had regained his footing behind the foggy screen. The ram was better than either of us had expected, measuring 37 inches around the curl with bases of $13^1/2$ inches. The fact that he wasn't the best ram we had seen made us wonder just how big some of the other sheep were.

After pictures, we took the cape, horns and meat down to our camp, and then re-packed everything for the hike down the glacier to an airstrip about a mile away. We were hoping that we might be able to radio Paul as he performed his daily fly-overs later in the day. A half hour after we arrived at the strip, that's exactly what happened. Paul swooped in and, one at a time, ferried us back to the lodge. I even arrived just in time for supper and a much-anticipated reunion with Janet. By the sounds of it, she had enjoyed a memorable week as well.

After our meal, I finally had a chance to clean up. The ulcers on both my ankles were the size of a quarter; it would take a month before the wounds healed completely. Janet and I were able to partake in several of the outfit's more interesting activities over the next couple of days, including a flight-seeing trip to the Bagley ice field. On August 26th, we headed back to Anchorage to catch the first flight of our journey home.

This was a tough hunt! Steve and I worked exceptionally hard, the mountains were unforgiving, and we endured a lot of bad luck. I had conquered the debilitating and painful wounds to both ankles and I had taken a very nice ram. That I had been unable to use the muzzleloader was a negative, as were the circumstances surrounding the sheep's death. Janet's presence was very much welcome, and I was pleased that her experience had been such a good one. Overall, the trip had met my expectations. Going forward, I fully expected to hunt sheep again, but I had no idea where the next stop on my sheep-hunting journey might land me.

Pilot and outfitter Paul Claus with his plane. I took this picture shortly after we landed on a glacier near the top of a mountain, depositing me and my equipment.

An un-named side glacier spills into the Hawkins glacier. The photo fails to adequately convey the irregular and undulating nature of the named glacier's surface.

This is me walking beneath the terminus of a glacier. Glaciers are pretty impressive!

Photo by Steve Johnson

A very nice Dall ram taken in the Wrangell Mountains of Alaska. We saw rams bigger than this one during our hunt. Note the rocky nature of the setting.

Photo by Steve Johnson

Dall Sheep—1998

Sheep hunting had become an important part of my life, but it wasn't the only thing that required my attention. My wife and I decided the time was right to build ourselves a new house, and the commitment to that project meant I wouldn't be making any trips to the mountains during 1997. By the following spring, the house was substantially complete and we had moved in, but plenty of finish work remained. Even though things were easing up, my preoccupation with the construction had left me little time or inclination to plan a hunt for 1998. However, I still felt the itch and as summer approached, I was increasingly on the prowl for any cancellation hunts that might place me back in sheep country.

Fortunately, I was presented with such an opportunity just in the nick of time. Another hunter was looking to unload his Dall sheep hunt in the Northwest Territories. If I was able to move quickly, I could go in his stead and save myself some money to boot. Flexibility wasn't a problem for me and, in short order, I had made all the necessary arrangements to arrive at the designated place on the appointed hour. Conditioning wasn't a concern either, as I had long since committed myself to maintaining year-round fitness. Except for the wintertime, I routinely walked with a heavy backpack even when I didn't have a hunt scheduled, just so I'd be able to take advantage of last-minute openings.

I would be hunting with Nahanni Butte Outfitters, owned by Cam and Clay Lancaster. The Lancaster's base camp wouldn't be the easiest hunting destination in North America to reach. The journey would take two full days and involve multiple modes of transportation. The first day of travel brought me to Edmonton, where I had to spend the night. From there, two more commercial flights were needed to reach Ft. Simpson, where the plane hit a goose as it landed. After collecting luggage, a two-hour drive followed by an hour-long boat ride down the Liard River finally landed me and some other clients at Nahanni Butte, the namesake of the outfit and the location of its base camp.

When traveling, firearms always made the trip more complicated. In the case of my muzzleloader, this fact of life was magnified several fold. If a center-fire rifle was lost in transit, it was altogether likely that my outfitter could lend me a suitable gun. If the airlines misplaced my black-powder gun, however, no like substitutes would be available. Besides that issue, getting black powder to the hunting area was a constant source of worry. It was preferable to have the outfitter obtain the needed propellant in advance of the hunt, but that wasn't always possible. Before September 11, 2001, I always managed to sneak small quantities of powder into out-of-the-way corners of my checked baggage; after that date, I didn't dare risk the consequences. Even if the gun and the powder which made it work arrived in camp, precautions had to be taken to ensure that the primitive firearm would discharge when it was supposed to. Moisture was a constant enemy, and great thought and care was devoted to keeping the powder dry and serviceable. And finally, once a shot had been taken, the muzzleloader had to be cleaned in a timely manner, lest the water-absorbing qualities of the powder rust the bore. For the entire duration of a hunting trip, there was never a time when I wasn't confronted with at least one of these worries.

The next day, my guide Keely Kibala and I were flown by small plane to an area bordering the Yukon, where the hunt would take place. Yet once more, I got sick on the flight and it took half a day to recover from the queasiness. Nevertheless, we went hunting; we even managed to find a group of seven rams, including one stalwart specimen. Late in the day we managed to stalk to within 200 yards of the group. Unable to advance further, we had to wait. Eventually, three of the rams fed down below us, but for some reason the rest of the band (including the big ram) went elsewhere. If the second group had followed the same path as the first three rams, we would have enjoyed some excitement. Instead, we just experienced a close call.

Keely and I initially erected our camp next to the airstrip, which was nothing more than a brushless piece of turf located on a flat plain some distance from the mountains. It wasn't like we were surrounded by sheep habitat, either. In fact, the nearby sheep haunts were fairly limited in scope and somewhat isolated. This was a significant departure from all the other areas I had hunted, but as long as we had rams to hunt, I didn't care. The terrain was rocky but not particularly problematic or dangerous. There were enough folds, nooks and crannies to hide sheep and make for a challenging hunt.

In an effort to cut several hours of walking off our daily routine, Keely and I moved our campsite closer to the mountain the next morning. Once the tent was in place, we quickly found the rams from the day before, not far from where we had left them the previous evening. We were able to work ourselves into position about 500 yards from the bedded sheep, but we just couldn't get closer. However, we were in a perfect place to ambush them if the rams chose to cross to the spot where we had initially seen them. As luck would have it, after ten hours of watching and waiting, when the sheep finally started feeding they walked higher and away from us.

As Keely and I left camp the next morning, we turned to see a grizzly bear running between us and the tent, about 100 yards away. Neither of us had any idea why the bear was in such a hurry, but we felt fortunate the bruin didn't discover our belongings and trash the whole camp. Once that excitement subsided, we continued our climb to the top, where we spotted two rams we hadn't seen before. They were positioned along the skyline further down the ridge.

Neither of the rams sported horns as impressive as the one we had been hunting for the previous two days, but both were big enough. The two of us cautiously continued towards the duo, but when we reached their last-known location, they had vanished. We continued our methodical search of the area and eventually discovered the rams feeding about 200 yards below. Unfortunately, just as we spied the rams, one of them noticed that something didn't quite look right. We froze, and after a long staring contest the rams relaxed and bedded.

Keely and I were caught in the relative open and we couldn't risk moving anywhere else. However, once we assumed a position low to the ground, the rock field we occupied provided enough concealment to prevent our detection. A very long standoff ensued. After staying in place for hours, the rams finally began to stir around 4:30pm. After a couple of false starts, the rams finally walked behind a small knoll, allowing us to rise and move towards them.

Lowering my profile as much as possible, I crawled to the top of the hill. Peeking through the tall grass at the knoll's crest, I could see a ram's head looking back in my direction. He must have caught some movement or heard an errant sound. After a couple of heart-pounding minutes, the ram relaxed his stare and turned his head to check on something else. Recognizing the opportunity, I immediately assumed a sitting position on the top of the knoll, found the ram's vitals and silently brought the hammer back. After fine-tuning my aim I pulled the trigger.

Even before the muzzle blast echoed back off the next mountain, I knew my bullet had missed its mark! In my eagerness to see the projectile's effect on the ram, I failed to maintain my concentration on the sights until after the gun had discharged. Instead, I peeked at the sheep just as I was finishing my trigger pull, causing the bullet to fly well wide of the mark. The fact that I was only 75 yards from the ram made my failure all the more painful. For crying out loud, I had made longer—and more difficult—shots shooting offhand!

At that moment, I couldn't have been more disgusted with myself. The stalk contained equal elements of difficulty and excitement, and it had been successful. Keely and I had shown great patience and skill in closing the distance, but I had singlehandedly blown an easy shot which would have capped the hunt. Furthermore, this pathetic performance followed on the heels of a similar fiasco in Wyoming, the last time I took aim at an animal with my muzzleloader. What really aggravated me was the knowledge that, despite my extensive preparation, I had still executed poorly. It wasn't like I never touched my gun until a week before a hunt. I practiced from field positions all the time, pushing the upper limits of my capabilities, only to screw up on two shots I considered well within my comfort zone.

Keely and I spent the next couple of days searching for suitable rams to hunt. There was something peculiar about the way sheep came and went on this mountain. As I stated earlier, the available sheep habitat didn't extend endlessly in all directions; it was much more isolated. This was even more apparent when viewed from the top of the mountain, where the boundary between the Yukon and Northwest Territories ran. From there, the Yukon side of the border featured a smooth gradual slope to the far-away timber, exhibiting very few of the amenities a sheep would find attractive. Conversely, the side we were hunting was steep and rugged, and it appeared to contain all the goodies sheep find desirable. Nevertheless, sheep we had been seeing early in the hunt disappeared for days, while new animals continued to pop into view, seemingly out of thin air.

A couple of days after my missed shot, as Keely and I were completing our traverse of the mountain's upper reaches in search of rams, Keely spotted what he thought was a sheep bedded below us. He was only able to see a little bit of white, but his discovery warranted a closer look. We were located in the middle of a substantial rock field, and by exercising great care, we ultimately closed the distance to 250 yards. Just then, three small rams walked into view to our left, peering curiously in our direction. They weren't yet on full-alert, but they had been tipped off to our presence, probably by the noise we made. Naturally, we froze in place, and much to our relief the youngsters soon calmed down. Minutes later, the area below us came alive with sheep, including one very big ram.

Without knowing it, Keely and I had blundered into the band of seven rams we had pursued the first two days of the hunt and hadn't seen since. The big ram was completely unaware that we were above him as he paraded out into the open some 200 yards below. That was still too far for the black-powder gun, of course. Instead of milling about the area, the rams looked like they were about to head elsewhere. Keely had been carting around a .270 Winchester at his employer's insistence, and he quickly urged me to trade guns. I didn't need much arm twisting given my most recent performance with the muzzleloader and the grandeur of the ram. The prospect of aiming through a scope instead of a peep sight seemed pretty appealing given my immediate past history.

With the gun swap completed I worked the bolt to chamber a live round. I had to wait some seconds before the ram was clear of the other sheep, but once that occurred, I wasted no time getting on the trigger. The walking ram dropped at the first shot but struggled to his feet. A couple of additional—albeit unnecessary—rounds finished the job. Everything had happened so quickly and unexpectedly that the whole episode seemed surreal. Where hard work had failed, blind luck had dropped an easy opportunity into our laps. As it relates to hunting, I guess you never know what could happen!

The ram we killed was undoubtedly the boss of the area—the same one we had seen the first two days of the hunt. How he and his mates had relocated from their original hangout to this particular place without us seeing them would always remain a complete mystery! Unlike most Dall sheep, this ram's horns were configured more like that of a bighorn sheep. That is: the bases were heavy and the mass was maintained all the way to the horn tips, which had been substantially broomed back. A quick tally of annual growth rings put the monarch's age at $10^1/_2$ years old.

The ram had been killed high on the mountain, directly above our campsite. After a suitable number of photographs were taken and the edible meat salvaged, Keely and I descended to the valley. After adding the remainder of our gear to our burgeoning packs, we headed for the airstrip. The ram had fallen around 2:30pm, and we arrived at our destination around 7pm, with daylight to spare. After placing the cape in the creek to wash out the blood and setting up camp, Keely cooked some tasty sheep tenderloins for supper.

Keely and I had hoped the plane would overfly the area the next day. The pilot would undoubtedly take notice of our success, land and then ferry us back to base camp. Unfortunately, no plane was heard nor seen. By day's end, it started to rain—the first precipitation of the hunt. It poured all night and well into the next day. After sixteen long hours, we finally were able to climb out of the tent and stand. Still, no plane appeared!

We may have had our ram, but there was no salt to treat the cape. This was worrisome because salt applied to the raw skin kept the hair from slipping from the hide. The next day featured perfect weather, but nobody came looking for us. That made three full days of watching, waiting and complete boredom. Both of us figured something must have been seriously wrong for that amount of time to pass without assistance. Around noon of the fourth day I heard the unmistakable sound of an engine in the distance. Our ride had finally arrived! Shortly thereafter, Keely and I were surrounded by the relative plushness of the Nahanni Butte facilities, living the good life.

Over the next few days, I was able to enjoy some down time at base camp before leaving for home. I learned that the reason we hadn't seen a plane for so long was part weather-related and part mechanical problem. Other hunters had arrived in camp while I had been in the field, and they had their own transportation. Three brothers, co-owners of a large lumber company in Prince George, B.C., commandeered the company's Bell 407 helicopter to bring them directly to the Butte, as well as ferry them about the hunting area. The brothers were originally from Slovenia and they knew how to have a good time. One night after dinner, they produced some alcoholic beverages that were shared with everyone present. Even though I'm not normally a drinker, I participated in one round of toasts, just to be polite.

I didn't know it when I left Canada, but in addition to my sheep horns and cape, I brought something else home with me. A couple of weeks after my hunt my health deteriorated. Specifically, I felt weak and I was having constant diarrhea, but the symptoms were subtlety different than anything I had previously experienced. Recalling the time I filled my water bottle from a stagnant pool, I began to suspect that I might have contracted giardiasis. When my symptoms didn't improve I sought medical attention, which confirmed my suspicions. With the appropriate treatment, I quickly recovered.

All things considered, my hunt with Nahanni Butte Outfitters had been a good experience. I met some very nice people, and I managed to take a fabulous ram. The three and a half days I spent waiting for the plane to show up almost drove me nuts, but insofar as the physical effort required, this was one of my easier hunts. Most hunters would have been thrilled with the outcome, and although I was pleased, I knew I still had some issues to contend with.

I had come to the Northwest Territories to take a respectable ram with my muzzleloader. In that, I had failed. The ram I killed, although substantially larger in horn than the one I had missed, was merely a consolation prize—a gift from the hunting gods. Given a choice, my clear preference would have been for the hard-earned ram with the smaller horns, cleanly taken with a primitive weapon. I knew I had performed poorly when it counted most, and that bothered me. If I was to continue hunting with the muzzleloader, I was going to have to make myself more proficient in the clutch.

This mountain provided most of the available sheep habitat for the hunt.

As seen here, the Northwest Territory side of the mountain we hunted featured an abundance of rock; the Yukon side of the hill was markedly more gentle.

This heavy-horned Dall sheep was taken in the Northwest Territories of Canada.

Desert Bighorn Sheep—1999

In the wake of my latest Dall sheep hunt, I did some serious soul searching regarding my hunting goals. With the house-building project behind me, I felt less constrained than I had for the past two years. As I mentally thrashed over the various possibilities, I finally realized that what really captivated me was obtaining a Grand Slam® with my muzzleloader. I was half way there, but realizing my goal would require two more hunts, assuming everything went well. Furthermore, unless I was to draw another permit, both hunts would be expensive.

I had hunted bighorns before, striking out both times. I hadn't yet experienced a hunt in the desert. The novelty of a unique setting, combined with the added bonus of being able to bring my wife along, convinced me to book a hunt in old Mexico. As a way of facilitating logistical issues, such as governmental firearms permits and mitigating my exposure to marginal outfitters, I made the arrangements through the Trophy Connection, a respected booking agency in Wyoming. The actual hunt would take place in the state of Sonora on a private ranch owned by Ivan Flores, an attorney in Hermosillo.

I worked my tail off preparing for the upcoming hunt, scheduled for November. From what I'd heard from hunters who'd been there, the hunting in Sonora was pretty cushy compared to practically every other sheep-hunting destination in North America. Comfortable ranch houses and fabulous food were the norm, and vehicles were routinely used to access the sheep habitat. Nevertheless, I didn't dare back off my fitness regimen.

What concerned me most, though, was my shooting ability. I was determined that this hunt would end differently than the last two times I had hunted with the black-powder gun, so I redoubled my efforts to establish shooting proficiency and confidence. As the hunt approached, I felt like I was right where I needed to be. Then, a couple of weeks before we were scheduled to fly to Mexico, disaster struck! My gun suddenly stopped shooting. One week the gun's point of impact and its ability to shoot consistent groups was fine; the next week I was lucky if I could hit the box the target was stapled to. I checked the obvious things that could lead to such a dramatic reduction in reliability, such as loose sights and action screws, but I couldn't isolate the cause. Out of desperation, I had a gunsmith examine the gun. Apparently, a badly pitted bore was responsible for the gun's sudden lack of consistency.

Just like that, everything I had been doing to build confidence was down the toilet. Fortunately, I had the option of replacing my ailing weapon with another of the same make and model, borrowed from a hunting buddy. However, I didn't have the time to develop the same level of trust and familiarity I had enjoyed with the gun that had killed my two previous sheep. Swapping guns at this late hour also presented potential problems with the Mexican authorities, who strictly supervised the entrance of firearms into their country. Some fast-stepping by Mr. Flores and the folks at the Trophy Connection produced an amended permit that would enable me to bring the substitute gun into the country. I zeroed the black-powder replacement with the bullets I normally used, and hoped for the best. I had always planned on bringing my .300 Winchester magnum as a second gun, just in case. With things as they were, that decision was looking wiser by the minute.

Janet and I left for Mexico on November 19th. Ivan met us at the Hermosillo airport and helped facilitate our passage through Mexican Customs. After a two-hour drive, we arrived at Ivan's Punta de Cirios ranch, which was bordered by the Sea of Cortez to the west. Ivan explained that the ranch had been named for an indigenous type of cactus which existed nowhere else. The staff was large and friendly, and the accommodations were super. Though tired from the long day of travel, I couldn't wait to start hunting in the morning.

I soon discovered that this experience would be quite different than all my previous sheep hunts. With a couple of exceptions, my prior hunts had two participants—me and my guide. However, the Mexicans utilized an entire group in the quest for game. One guide was in charge, but several subordinates aided in the search for sheep. In my case, a young man named Martín was the head honcho, while Jorge and Lazlo assisted. Ivan even came along the first day.

The ranch contained many dirt roads, and a jeep was used to access key glassing locations. If no animals were spotted from one place, all of us would hop back into the vehicle and we would drive to another observation point. Although the mornings were cool, the daytime temperatures could hit eighty. Finally, while raingear had been a constant companion on my previous hunts, it wasn't going to be needed here in the desert.

In its own unique way, the desert was every bit as beautiful as the northern terrain I was more accustomed to. Snow and ice had been replaced by sand, but the landscape wasn't bare by any means. Actually, vegetation existed everywhere. Nothing grew very tall, and almost every plant contained thorns, spines or barbs of one sort or another. Leather work gloves were worn to help protect hands from the ever-present sharpies. Several types of cacti could be found, including saguaro, cholla, prickly pear, barrel and pipe. Palo verde, mesquite, yucca and ocotillo were some of the other trees, shrubs and plants present in abundance.

As I surveyed the larger hunting area, it was apparent that the available sheep habitat was confined to a spine of mountainous terrain that ran roughly north to south, parallel to the nearby coast of the Sea of Cortez. The blue sea was never more than a mile distant. From sea level, the mountains jutted skyward more than a thousand feet. Colored predominately in shades of tan with tinges of red in places, the peaks were impressive but they didn't appear to be particularly formidable. Looking eastward, the mountain tops abruptly receded to a flat desert plain, which continued as far as the eye could see.

The first two days of hunting followed a similar pattern. We'd all rise early, eat breakfast and then drive to a promising lookout to glass for sheep, in the hope that we'd catch rams while they were still on the move. When no rams were discovered from our initial location, we'd move elsewhere and continue our search. Around noon, it was time to head back to the ranch house for lunch and a siesta, thereby avoiding the hottest—and least productive—hours of the day. Later in the afternoon, we'd go check for sheep from some vantage points we hadn't visited earlier.

Before the sun came up it was quite cool, but it didn't take long to warm into the seventies. The mid-day break gave me a chance to visit with Janet, who amused herself at the ranch, mostly by reading. Although we'd occasionally climb a small hill to get a better look at the visible sheep habitat, I certainly wasn't killing myself physically. The food Natcho, the on-site chef, prepared couldn't have been better. Fresh shrimp and halibut were just two of the more notable entrees. As advertised, this was proving to be the easiest sheep hunt I'd ever taken.

For me, the allure of Mexico wasn't to be found in the food or the relative effortlessness of the hunt. Those things were nice, but I was there to kill a desert sheep, first and foremost. And so far, despite the fact that the ranch was reportedly home to over 200 animals, sheep were a scarce commodity. We were seeing a couple of animals here and there, but mature rams were notably absent. Finally, just before dark on the second day of hunting, a small group of rams was spotted. Although there wasn't enough daylight remaining to immediately stalk the sheep, we had reason to be optimistic about what the next morning might bring.

We had no trouble locating the rams early the next day. As we expected, they hadn't moved very far. In all, there were three rams. The largest of the bunch was respectable, but he wasn't one of the giants I had been hearing about. Around 10:30am, convinced that the rams would stay bedded for a while, Martín, Lazlo and I began our stalk. Jorge stayed at the jeep. As we neared the ridgeline the rams occupied, I began to fear that our approach would place us upwind of the sheep. Sure enough, when we peeked over the ridge the sheep were gone. From his station, Jorge saw the rams running flat out for the next country, our scent still in their nostrils.

I've always felt that the stalk is one of the more problematic aspects of hunting sheep. From a distant vantage point it's pretty easy to pick a route which will take you to a suitable ambush site. The problem is: once you leave that vantage point, nothing ever looks quite the same. Unless unique and unmistakable landmarks exist to guide your progress, the unvarying nature of the terrain makes it pretty easy to veer off course. Many times, a small miscalculation in travel amounts to little more than an inconvenience; on this occasion, ending up on the wrong side of the sheep was a mission-critical mistake.

In this particular instance, my bearings had been more

accurate than those of the Mexicans. However, knowing that failure was imminent and communicating the same was a problem. Martín spoke a little English and I was minimally conversant in Spanish. Neither of us was equipped to carry on an intricate discussion regarding route-finding in the other's primary language. And so, I let the guides do the guiding and hoped I would be wrong about the outcome. Unfortunately, I wasn't!

The next three days were a repeat of the first pair of hunting days, except that we did a lot more walking. Glassing from the roads hadn't proven very productive, so we felt we might have a better chance of finding some sheep if we "got in among 'em," so to speak. We even split into two groups on occasion in an attempt to cover more ground. Though we found sheep every day, mature rams were nowhere to be seen. I could tell that this fact of life was weighing heavily on Martín and the others. They knew good rams resided on the ranch, yet our collective efforts had failed to produce a single sighting. After six days of hunting, we only had a single encounter with a marginal ram, and that episode had ended in failure. Everyone was feeling the pressure.

Suddenly, a hunt that had been advertised as 100% successful was down to its last two days. On November 26th, Martín found another marginal ram which we decided to pursue. In complete conformity with the way things had been going, though, we were never able to approach within a mile of the ram. On the final day of hunting, I carried the .300 Winchester. Martín found a ram but he wasn't sure of his size. The two of us moved closer for a better look, eventually narrowing the distance to 300 yards. The ram was immature and small of horn. It would have been perfectly legal for me to kill the youngster, but as I looked through the scope, I just couldn't pull the trigger. I decided I just didn't need a desert sheep that badly. I've made plenty of mistakes in my hunting career, but letting that ram walk wasn't one of them! The hunt was over.

Perhaps the highlight of the trip had been the fabulous Thanksgiving dinner that Ivan had arranged for us. Complete with turkey, mashed potatoes and the fixings, the feast was as good as any we had ever enjoyed at home. Away from our families on this quintessential American holiday, Janet and I were both touched by the thoughtfulness of our host and thankful for the friendship of those present.

Our time depleted, Janet and I returned home, but not before Ivan insisted that I come back to hunt later in the season. He had never had a hunter fail to get a sheep, and he didn't want to break that streak. I didn't relish the prospect of making another trip—this time alone—but I didn't enjoy being skunked without even an opportunity for a shot, either. Besides that, the hunt was expensive and I hadn't gotten my money's worth. In short order, arrangements were made for another go at these elusive desert bighorns, starting on December 19th.

My return hunt would take place at another of Ivan's ranches, further down the coastline. Leading up to my departure, the ranch hands had been seeing two good rams every day on the mountain bordering the ranch house. As I started my journey, that knowledge spurred some renewed optimism on my part. I was also looking forward to seeing some new country. Martín met me at the airport in Hermosillo, and we quickly set off for the ranch by car.

The route was a little different than before, taking us through the coastal town of Kino Bay. From there, Tiburon Island looms large in the Sea of Cortez as you look westward. Martín and I arrived in Kino just as the sun was setting, and the view was one of the most spectacular I have ever witnessed. The sky was awash in varying shades of red and orange. There were just enough high-level clouds present to give the scene an interesting texture that only served to enhance the visual appeal.

The next morning, just like clockwork, the two rams the ranch hands had been seeing for a string of days were observed well up on the mountain next to the ranch house. Speaking of mountains, this one was a giant. Named in honor of the American surveyor who charted it, Pico Johnson rose over 3,000 feet above the nearby sea. Unlike the shorter and less impressive peaks of Punta de Cirios, this mountain was steep, extremely rugged and thick with vegetation. The soil exhibited a distinct red hue.

Once it was determined that the two rams had settled down for the day, Martín, Jorge and I readied ourselves for the trip up the mountain. Lazlo, who had been present in November, was out of commission with a bad knee. As I started to remove my muzzleloader from the gun case, Martín waved me off. He explained that he didn't think it was possible to get within muzzleloader range in this particular environment. As I surveyed the landscape, I found it difficult to fault his assessment. And even though Martín didn't bring it up, my appraisal of the situation told me that this was a do-or-die attempt. I realized that if we spooked the sheep, we'd never see those rams again. They would disappear into some brush-clogged and inaccessible ravine for the remainder of the hunt. That prospect, reinforced by fresh memories of our poor luck on my previous trip, gave me pause. Without even putting up a fight, I took the .300 Winchester out of the case and grabbed some ammo. Even though I selected the weapon with a longer reach, given what was before us, I still thought we'd need some luck to get a shot at one of the rams.

The three of us drove to the backside of the mountain and started our climb. The plan was to use the mountain to hide our movement until we had reached an elevation well above the rams, then cross a ridgeline back onto the flank of the hill the sheep occupied. This meant the rams would be out of our sight for some time. Hopefully, they wouldn't move very far, if at all, during the intervening hours. If the rams were up and moving, we would likely see them from our new vantage point; if not, we could use the terrain to conceal our approach to their last-known location.

The climb was long, steep and torturous—at least 1,500 feet in all. The dry ravines we utilized were thick with brush and nasty. Eventually, we reached a narrow bench which afforded us a pathway to the rams' side of the mountain. Before going further, we used the shade to recuperate from our exertions. As I ate lunch, three feet from my right elbow, a precipitous drop-off left nothing but empty space for at least 800 vertical feet. Reinvigorated, the three of us began our descent towards the sheep, which couldn't yet be seen due to the steepness of our surroundings.

The climb to the bench had been a real grunt. Getting down to the rams wouldn't be much easier, and the trip would prove to be far more dangerous. Initially, I doubted it was even possible to get from where we were to where we wanted to go. The terrain was as hellacious as any I had ever been exposed to. If not for the brush, which we used continuously to maintain balance and avert a fall, we wouldn't have made it down in one piece. Even so, Martín lost his footing and fell twice. Fortunately, he didn't slide far and he wasn't hurt in the process. On multiple occasions, Martín would carefully lower himself through a tricky section of rock and ledge, whereupon I would hand the rifle down to him before following his path. That way, both my hands would be free to steady myself.

After painstakingly descending about 200 vertical yards in this manner, we stopped to regroup. The rams were still out of sight below us, but we were getting closer. In an effort to reduce the noise we made, Martín and I removed our packs and left our non-essential gear with Jorge before continuing lower. After another hundred yards of harrowing down-climbing, we approached the remaining ledge which concealed the sheep from view. We quietly inched our way to the crest, exposing just enough of our heads to look into the thicket below. Almost immediately, a ram was seen standing in the brush at the bottom of the cliff. We had the element of surprise, but we didn't yet have a clear shot. Ducking out of sight, we advanced a few yards along the ledge and then re-emerged above the ram. This time, I had an unobstructed view of the sheep, which was facing directly away from me—a measly twenty-five yards below! The ram never knew what hit him.

Almost immediately, the air was filled with the sounds of whopping and hollering Mexicans, as Martín, followed by Jorge, and then by a couple of ranch hands down on the road, celebrated a successful hunt in their own unique style. Just as quickly, Martín turned to me and began apologizing for stopping me from bringing the muzzleloader. Obviously, he had misjudged our chances of getting black-powder close to the rams, but it was I who had made the final decision regarding which gun to carry. Accordingly, I immediately did what I could to relieve Martín of whatever guilt he may have harbored, while assuring him that I was pleased by the outcome.

The dead ram may have been only a couple dozen yards away, but working our way to him wasn't any easier than the rest of the stalk had been. Jorge brought down the rest of our gear, and the ranch hands quickly climbed to our level to join in the festivities. It was quite apparent that killing a sheep was a real big deal to all the guys, no matter what their role might have been. And everyone wanted to be included in the numerous photographs that were taken.

After the picture taking was completed, I requested that the ram be caped for a life-size mount. The bullet had exited the brisket between the two front legs, testifying to the fact that the shooting angle had been almost straight down. The ram was obviously older, but his horns weren't huge. That mattered little, however, as I was pleased to have taken a mature animal. A wart-like growth in the middle of his Roman nose, probably the result of previous head-butting contests with other rams, added to the dead ram's character, and the cape was colored a beautiful shade of gray.

Once the ram had been reduced to parts, we started down towards the road. I proudly carried the horns and hide despite the repeated offers of help from the Mexicans. Once we extricated ourselves from the rat hole where the sheep had come to rest, the remainder of the descent wasn't too difficult. Upon reaching the road, I turned to examine the path we had taken to reach the ram. From this perspective, our journey seemed just as impossible as it had when viewed from above. The ram had been killed around 1pm, and we arrived at the ranch house at 4:30pm. In short order, a bottle of tequila was produced, initiating a series of toasts in celebration of a successful hunt. I gave homage to 'el borrego' (ram in Spanish) and my new friends. The festivities seemed incomplete without Lazlo's presence, though.

Ivan called and offered his congratulations, and he pledged to rearrange my flights home. We were to meet him in his office at 10am the next day. The ride to Hermosillo featured two flat tires and a vehicle swap, but Martín and I arrived just a half hour later than expected. The paperwork which would allow me to import my animal into the United States was in order, and Ivan had even managed to reschedule my flights for later in the day. After a refreshing soda and some pleasant conversation, Martín brought me to the airport. Just that quickly, my whirlwind trip to Mexico was over, and I was on my way home.

Unlike my first journey to Mexico, the second visit was short, sweet and successful. My return had certainly erased the disappointment I felt subsequent to the first go-around, not to mention the fact that it kept Ivan's unblemished record intact. As is often the case when hunting, a single spectacular day had supplanted more than a week of hard luck and frustration. I had taken a fine desert bighorn at the conclusion of the most physically challenging stalk I had ever been involved in.

I had good cause to be proud, yet I hadn't fulfilled my original goal. Martín and I had approached the ram closely enough to have killed him with my muzzleloader, an arrow or maybe even with a perfectly thrown rock. However, I had allowed worldly cares to break down my resolve to remain exclusively a muzzleloader hunter. My desire to return home in time for Christmas influenced my thinking, as did the cost of the hunt, our long run of bad luck and the prospect of failure. Perhaps the final consideration was the unproven replacement gun I had been forced to put into service. At this stage of my development, I wasn't fully capable of disregarding these pressures. Success, when measured solely in terms of dead animals, is a result-driven temptress who cares little about methods. I had hedged my bets and chosen to maximize my chances of taking a ram, and I had done so at the expense of the larger goal of accomplishing the feat with a primitive weapon.

Despite these feelings, I didn't brood about not killing the ram with my black-powder gun; I just accepted the outcome for what it was, and hoped the experience would make me a better hunter in the future. I was grateful for the opportunity to harvest a very nice desert sheep and for the kindness and friendship of the hard-working Mexicans. All in all, the hunt provided some very special memories.

Pico Johnson near the Sea of Cortez. This mountain served as the setting for my return hunt to Mexico in December 1999.

Jorge (l) and Martin (r) with my first desert sheep, taken in Sonora, Mexico.

ROCKY MOUNTAIN BIGHORN SHEEP— 2003

The desert sheep hunt in Mexico had stretched my resources, and that necessitated a hiatus from the mountains in order to replenish my bank account. As proof of my self-restraint, I had planned to abstain from hunting sheep for the next two seasons. But for various reasons, an additional year would pass before I would hunt the high country again. In the interim, I kept myself in top shape in case the right cancellation hunt became available. That never happened, but for something different, I went to Argentina to climb the tallest mountain outside of the Himalayas in January of 2002. Aconcagua rose nearly 23,000 feet in the Andes Mountains, and although bad weather kept me from reaching the summit, I experienced some real high-altitude adventure.

Part of the reason for my longer-than-expected absence from sheep hunting was the loss of my trusted muzzleloader. Before the hunt in Mexico, I had decided to pursue my Grand Slam® with a black-powder gun. Of course, that goal had been compromised almost immediately when my gun abruptly stopped performing. The fact that I subsequently shot the desert sheep with a rifle left me with two problems: In order to complete my muzzleloader slam I would need to find another primitive weapon which could be relied upon, and I would need to pay for yet another desert bighorn hunt.

Booking the hunt would be straightforward but expensive. Finding a replacement for my worn-out muzzleloader would prove to be much more difficult than expected. I bought another Thompson/Center product called the Black Mountain Magnum, also in .54 caliber. Unfortunately, the gun was nothing but trouble. As soon as I opened the box, I noticed that the lug which was used to secure the barrel to the stock wasn't peened in place and freely slid out of its dovetail. I sent the gun back to the factory to have that defect repaired. Once that was taken care of, I attempted to find a bullet/powder combination which would shoot consistent groups. No matter what I tried—and I experimented with many different variations—I could never achieve the kind of precision I thought was needed to hunt sheep. Hell, I wasn't even that comfortable using the gun to hunt deer, where the shots were rarely longer than fifty yards.

Without a dependable primitive weapon, I couldn't commit myself to a sheep hunt, and time slipped by as I struggled to make things work. More than that, though, my goals, which had only come into focus immediately prior to the hunt in Mexico, were thrown into disarray. Eventually, my desire to hunt sheep again, fueled by an unexpectedly long absence, prodded me to action. With only one sheep remaining to complete a Grand Slam® with a center-fire rifle, a hunt for a Rocky Mountain bighorn became the obvious choice for my next adventure. My .300 Winchester magnum would be pressed into service.

For some time, I had been a member of Carter's Hunters Services (no relation), a Utah-based hunting consultant company. Their monthly magazine helped me submit my annual applications for sheep permits in the western states in a timely manner. I contacted one of their recommended outfitters in Alberta, Canada. Kendall Johnson, owner of Mountain's Edge Outfitting, hunted sheep in the Willmore Wilderness Park in west-central Alberta, just north of Jasper National Park. Satisfied with the hunt particulars, I booked a bighorn hunt for mid-September.

My itinerary included stops in Toronto and Calgary before reaching my final destination of Grande Prairie. Kendall met me at the airport and we drove two hours south to his home in Grande Cache. The next two days were spent lounging around as Kendall attended to last-minute preparations for the hunt, including shoeing his string of horses. On September 13th, we began the nearly ten-hour ride to our camp deep in the Willmore. For me, that's an extremely long time in the saddle. Besides giving me a sore rear end, riding a horse really wrecks my knees. I guess I'm just not bow-legged enough. To save my legs, I led the horse for about a third of the trip. Just before dark, we reached the cabin which would serve as the base of operations for the hunt.

Besides Kendall, there were others involved in the hunt. A young man named Owen served as an assistant guide, and he normally accompanied us while hunting unless other duties required his attention. Jay wrangled horses and Becky kept everyone well fed. A couple of days later, our ranks would swell with the additions of Kendall's nephew Brett and Bernie, the hunter he would be guiding.

The scenery in the vicinity of the cabin, which was located in a high alpine meadow, was pretty. The lower elevations, dominated by willows, alders and spruce, held decent populations of elk and mule deer, while the high country was home to sheep and mountain goats. Typical of bighorn habitat, the surrounding peaks contained timber, but much of the terrain was open and bare of significant vegetation. According to Kendall, we would use the horses for day hunts to the closest sheep country, and if those spots didn't pan out, we could relocate the base of operations to more remote areas.

The first three days of hunting were uneventful. In fact, for two of those days we never left camp. Rain, low clouds and horizontal snow alternately worked to make for impossible glassing conditions. On the plus side, at least we were stationed in a warm cabin instead of a colder, flimsier and more confining tent. Kendall, Owen and I traveled about two hours to explore a mountainous area which featured big open basins on September 17th. The country was grand, but the trail we used left a lot to be desired. Short spruce trees continually pulled at the stirrups, twisting my knees in the process. By the end of the day, my left knee not only hurt when I rode, but it also pained me when walking.

The next day, the three of us left the cabin and made a move to a new area. It took half a day to pack up the horses and the rest of the day to get to the new location. Hunting-wise, the day was a waste of time. At least the ride didn't seem to make my knee any worse. The plan was to spend the next several days backpacking in the surrounding country. Hopefully, we'd finally find some sheep. To this point, all we'd seen was a single ewe. In any event, at least my knees would get a break from riding.

On September 19th, Kendall and I left Owen and our impromptu camp and climbed higher. The camp was located in a protected valley, but upon gaining the ridge we were met by an unexpectedly ferocious wind. The higher elevations also held significant snowfall in places, which made for slippery walking. Despite having to deal with difficult conditions we did see sixty sheep, although no mature rams were among them.

The following day Kendall and I headed in a different direction, and we covered a lot of ground in the process. Much of our travels encompassed steep side hills covered by thick patches of stunted spruce trees, which made for uneven walking and difficult footing. In these situations, I couldn't always see where to place my feet, so it became necessary to "feel" my way through the thickets. Sometimes my foot would hit solid ground or a stout limb; other times I'd drop into hole and have to extricate myself. We must have given six or seven different basins a thorough glassing, but we couldn't find a single sheep. We looked at a lot of really nice sheep habitat, too.

On the third day of hunting from this camp, Kendall and I returned to the area where we had seen all the sheep two days earlier. We had no trouble finding a large bunch of lambs and ewes, but rams were once again absent. The highlight of the day came when I spotted a grizzly bear high on the slope of an adjoining mountain, well above the sheep we had been watching. The bear eventually decided to descend to the valley, which set off a sense of semi-panic among the heretofore calm sheep. One group of lambs and ewes climbed high onto the hillside facing us, while another contingent sought safety in the jagged peaks where we were situated. The sheep were unaware of our presence and they passed within yards of us. The way sheep move about the treacherous heights has always been a source of fascination—and jealousy—for me.

Having found nothing worth hunting, the plan was to leave the area the next day. It rained during the night and into the morning. We awoke to find that some of the horses had left before us. The only way to feed them was to let them eat what grew naturally around the camp. And even though the steeds were routinely hobbled in an effort to prevent them from wandering too far away, hobbles would only slow—not stop—a determined horse. To make a long story short, the horses were recovered but I spent over three hours in the rain watching over two tied mounts while Kendall and Owen rounded up the wayward animals. I also ended up walking with a full pack for another three hours, while only riding one hour. By nightfall, everyone was back at the cabin, tired and soaked. Brett and Bernie were there also, and they hadn't seen a ram yet, either.

For the next two days Kendall and I hunted from the cabin. On the first day, it was noon before the horses were readied for the hunt. Everyone except Becky was headed elsewhere. That meant the entire string of horses had to first be gathered, and then packed or saddled before we could leave. Tending to that many horses was time-consuming. Finally underway, Kendall and I headed up a valley we had explored earlier in the hunt. The weather was ideal and we saw a dozen sheep, but no rams, in an abbreviated day. At this stage of the hunt, the total lack of rams was worrisome. The second day, we headed up the same valley, but continued our journey well beyond the stopping point from the day before. In total, that amounted to about a twelve-mile round trip on foot for me, as I rode very little in an attempt to protect my knees.

Finally, though, we found some rams. Kendall happened to be glassing a ridge when a couple of rams popped onto the skyline for a few minutes before dropping back into the basin on the far side. They were a long way away, and they were visible so briefly that trophy potential couldn't be determined. But two rams were definitely there, and it was possible that others were nearby but had escaped our detection. The odds of a legal ram being present were good enough to warrant further investigation on our part. The remaining question was one of timing.

Kendall and I only had a few hours of daylight left to us, and we had neither a tent nor sleeping bags. Returning to the cabin would allow us to gather those items and any other supplies we might need to camp in the vicinity of the rams and hunt them for several days. Since we felt that the rams were unlikely to move far, we opted to go back to the cabin for the night, stock up and return in the morning. All things considered, that plan seemed more likely to result in success than making a mad rush for the rams so late in the day. Time would tell.

The next morning, Owen accompanied us to the place where we had seen the rams. After Kendall and I collected our gear, Owen trailed the horses back to the cabin. That way, we wouldn't have to worry about the mounts. Owen would return in a couple of days to pick us up. Hopefully, we'd have a ram by then. Kendall and I had about 1,500 feet of climbing ahead of us, so I stripped down to the bare minimum to avoid getting soaked with sweat. The uphill effort wasn't as bad as I had anticipated, but once we ascended above the timber we were met by forty-mile-per-hour winds. Even with the extra weight of a full pack, I couldn't even place my feet where I wanted. Each time I attempted to set my foot down on a particular rock, the force of the wind would push me off course, increasing the chances of a twisted ankle or a fall.

Despite the wind, Kendall and I finally made it to the top and began our search for the rams. They weren't in exactly the same spot as they had been one day earlier, but they hadn't moved far. Now that we had the rams located, we quickly found an inconspicuous campsite near the top of the mountain and set up the tent. That job accomplished, we devoted the last hour of daylight to attempting to get within range of the rams. Unfortunately, they were feeding in an open basin which wouldn't allow us to approach any closer than 500 yards. We slipped back to the tent, ate supper and went to bed, hopeful that we'd have a better opportunity in the morning.

During the night, it seemed as though the wind would destroy the tent. Between the constant shaking and the noisy reverberations which accompanied it, sleep was impossible.

By 7am, Kendall and I were headed to the basin that held the rams. They were still there, but for most of the day they were no more approachable than they had been the night before. A long cold vigil would ensue.

While Kendall and I waited for a change in circumstances, we passed the time with various diversions. The day was cold and keeping warm was of the essence. Fortunately, under cover of a nearby ravine, we could climb periodically to restore circulation to fingers and toes. I used stones to dam up a section of the gully so we could collect melting snow in our water bottles. We even saw a wolverine scamper across a shale slide a couple of hundred yards away. During our wait we had plenty of opportunities to carefully examine the sheep. As it turned out, there were only two rams and they were accompanied by a few ewes. Only one of the rams was judged to be legal.

The group had spent the day at the far end of the large basin. Finally, around 2:30pm, the sheep rose from their beds and began working their way towards us. The basin narrowed substantially near its mouth, where Kendall and I were positioned. We were hidden in some rocks about half way down one flank of the basin. If the rams continued on course, I couldn't envision a scenario where I wouldn't get a decent shot.

As they advanced, I prepared myself for the long-awaited opportunity. I had already taken readings from my rangefinder to ascertain the distances to noteworthy landmarks. Next, I performed all the small essential tasks leading up to a shot: chamber a live round, remove the scope cover, make spare ammo available, and build a steady shooting position. Once a ram was within range, all that remained was to adjust the sight picture to correct for the shooting angle and distance, control my breathing and flip off the safety. Kendall's job was to direct me to the legal ram.

Completely unaware of the danger, the sheep continued in our direction at a steady pace. Before long, the legal ram passed by a rock which I had ranged at 250 yards. Assured that he was within comfortable shooting distance, I now had the ram in my scope, waiting only for him to turn broadside. He ran to one of the ewes, sniffed at her rear end and stood for a moment. The cross hairs were steady, so I exhaled before gently pulling the trigger. At the shot, the ram dropped in his tracks and never even twitched. I had my first bighorn in three tries, as well as my Grand Slam®!

The quick clean kill washed a lot of tension off the mountain, for me and for Kendall. I was happy, sad and overwhelmed, but mostly, I was relieved. Seventeen days had passed since I left home, hunting days were dwindling and the dead ram was the only legal sheep we had seen. Kendall and I enjoyed a celebratory moment; I even took a drag from his half-consumed cigarette. As we waited for the other sheep to slowly file off, I put the rangefinder on the ram's lifeless body. The instrument indicated that he laid 220 yards away.

Kendall and I worked our way down to the valley to view our prize. The ram was large of body but small of horn. I'd be lying if I said I wouldn't have preferred an older ram with larger horns. The dead ram's buddy fit that description, but according to Alberta's game regulations, he wasn't legal. By the grace of God, I had been placed in a position which would have allowed me to shoot either ram; I took the one which would pass muster with the game warden, and I was proud to have done so.

The bullet had blasted through both shoulders, destroying the lungs in the process. Plenty of pictures were taken before the knives came out. Kendall took enough cape for a shoulder mount, and then we turned our attention to salvaging the meat. Due to bullet placement some meat was lost, but we retrieved all we could. After loading our packs, we climbed back up the ravine to our camp. That effort wasn't as tough as I had expected. Once there, I ate supper before turning in for the night. For the third consecutive meal, the entrée consisted of a single granola bar.

Kendall and I rose at first light, struck the tent and packed everything for the trip down the mountain. Descending with heavy packs is always hard work, and it tends to cause blistered feet. We were careful and three hours later we arrived safely at our prior drop-off point. Owen was expected to return at 2pm, so we had some time to kill. Kendall used the time to finish preparing the cape. Owen arrived on schedule, and the three of us made it to the cabin around 5pm. A shower wasn't available, but the chili supper Becky made for us really hit the spot, especially in light of the deprivation of the last three days.

Our trek back to civilization began early the following morning, and it didn't start well. Kendall was in a foul mood, and while attempting to pack one of the horses he became displeased with the steed's behavior. Predictably, a series of kicks and whippings with the reins only served to cause the horse to rear and buck violently. As I watched in dismay, off flew my sheep horns and my pack which landed at the horse's feet. I still don't know how the horns weren't trampled in the process. After a cooling-down period, the horses were finally readied for the journey back to town.

The ride out wasn't without problems, either, but we made it to the trailhead in just under nine hours. Actually, I walked most of the way to save my ailing knees and my butt. In total, I rode less than two hours, but I was glad that I limited my time in the saddle. Back at Kendall's house, the atmosphere calmed considerably and Becky put together another fine meal, this time featuring back straps from my sheep. I also had the chance to remove two weeks of excess facial hair and accumulated grunge.

Before I could leave for home, we still had to have the horns checked and plugged by the Provincial authorities, and that occurred mid-afternoon of the next day. That accomplished, Brett drove me back to Grande Prairie. It was startling to see how much the trees had changed since my arrival. The aspens had been green, but while I had been hunting a transformation had occurred. The diminishing daylight and below-freezing temperatures had caused the leaves to turn golden yellow, giving the mountains enhanced contrast and beauty.

I was scheduled to fly home the following day, but when Brett and I arrived in Grande Prairie, I asked him to stop at the airport. That impulse was fortuitous, as I was able to catch a flight to Edmonton which left within the hour. I would have to overnight there, but by making that flight I also shaved seven hours of travel off my original itinerary. That suited me fine, as I was anxious to get back home. For someone accustomed to flight delays and postponements, having things go my way for a change felt pretty good.

The trip to Alberta had been lengthy but productive. I could now document the fact that I had taken each of the four species which constituted the Grand Slam® of North American wild sheep. I was proud of the achievement, but I also felt unfulfilled. What I really desired was to accomplish the same feat with my muzzleloader. Until that happened, as a means of keeping myself focused on what I considered to be my ultimate goal, I decided to defer the submission of my credentials to the Grand Slam® Club, widely recognized as the record-keeping authority on such matters.

A small pond in a high alpine plain. We used this location to glass for sheep on several occasions.

The beauty of Alberta—granite domes rising above timbered slopes.

My first Rocky Mountain bighorn after three tries. This ram completed my Grand Slam with a rifle.

Photo by Kendall Johnson

Marco Polo Sheep—2004

Subsequent to my bighorn hunt in Alberta, I attended the FNAWS convention in January as an unofficial Grand Slammer, and I was actively on the prowl for sheep hunts. I had pretty good luck, too. For the first time, I booked a hunt for each of the next two seasons. I scheduled a bighorn hunt in British Columbia for 2005, and a hunt in Kyrgyzstan for Marco Polo sheep for the coming November.

As my fascination with sheep had grown, I became aware that other places in the world contained sheep, most notably Asia, where numerous species of both wild sheep and goats resided. Perhaps the most famous, and arguably the most beautiful, of the world's sheep was the vaunted Marco Polo argali. Although they could also be found in China and Afghanistan, for all intents and purposes, the sport-hunting opportunities were confined to the central-Asian countries of Tajikistan and Kyrgyzstan. No matter where these sheep called home, they lived at very high altitudes—from 10,000 to 17,000 feet above sea level.

Named after the Venetian explorer, Marco Polo rams were significantly larger in body than even the Rocky Mountain bighorn of North America. Live weights exceeding 300 pounds were the norm. The sheep were generally light in color about the neck, legs and rump, but they exhibited brown pelage on their backs and sides. Without a doubt, though, the most impressive feature was their spiraling horns. A mature ram could grow horns which exceeded sixty inches in length. Besides being long, the horns assumed an attractive configuration. After rising from the skull, the horns arced downward, dropping well below the jaw line before turning upward again. As the horns rose from their low point, they dramatically tipped out to the sides. For the largest specimens, it was common for the tips of the horns to curl down and back near their terminations.

I had booked the hunt through hunting consultant Harv Holleck for November. I made a conscious decision to hunt in Kyrgyzstan rather than Tajikistan for the following reasons: it was easier (but not easy) to get to, the elevations weren't as high and the terrain wasn't quite as open. I was also influenced by the knowledge that someone I respected had been on this hunt previously and he was planning on making this trip. Since this was to be my first foray out of North America, I figured a seasoned hand would help me maneuver through the inevitable rough spots. Supposedly, the rut would be in full force and rams would be plentiful.

The itinerary was much longer than anything I had experienced to that point—New York to Istanbul, Turkey (10 hours), followed by seven hours of waiting in the airport, and then a six-hour flight from Istanbul to Bishkek, the capital of Kyrgyzstan. Of course, I had to get from my home to JFK airport in New York, and that effort required a ride in the car, a short flight and a shuttle bus from Newark—each of which took about an hour.

Upon landing in Bishkek, it was reassuring to see a fleet of U.S. Air Force C-130s lined up on the tarmac. Since the invasion of nearby Afghanistan, the United States had been using the airfield as a supply base for the war effort. Harv and his crew met me and a couple of other hunters as we cleared customs about 3am local time. The next stop was a hotel in downtown Bishkek. I hadn't been in bed two hours when the phone rang. In broken English, the female voice on the other end of the line introduced herself as the "sex massage lady." I politely declined in favor of something much more important—a decent night's sleep. Welcome to the third world!

The next day was spent recovering from all the travel and adapting to the ten-hour time difference. Harv showed me and the other hunters (Alan Maki, Al Butcher and Duane Sather) around the city. Kyrgyzstan was an Islamic country, but Bishkek had a decidedly western feel to it. Young people dominated the streets and the stores, and although the buildings weren't as fresh as the typical American mall, the emphasis on modern electronic goods wasn't that dissimilar. Harv said that many of the young women prostitute themselves to earn money to buy wares, go to school and find a way out of the country to a better life.

Everyone rose early the next day for the much-anticipated drive to our hunting camp. According to Harv, who would stay behind, we could expect approximately sixteen hours of fun. He also warned us that the record was twenty-nine hours. Variables such as how much snow covered the mountain passes and whether any tractor trailers were overturned in the road would ultimately determine the actual duration of the trip. The vehicles left a lot to be desired, but the roads were worse. Gravel was the dominant surface, and precipitous drop-offs were common near the mountain passes. We voluntarily stopped several times to eat and stretch our legs. On another occasion, we were pulled over for taking a shortcut, whereupon the official was paid a small bribe to let us continue on our way. Near the end of the trip, we encountered a military checkpoint, where a serious review of passports and firearms permits was undertaken. It was well after dark when we finally bounced into the hunting camp after a mere thirteen hours of travel.

The camp was situated at more than 10,000 feet above sea level, near the base of an extensive series of mountains in the Tien Shan Range. The Chinese border was less than twenty miles away, on the distant side of the mountains. The aforementioned military checkpoint was located twenty miles in the opposite direction, positioned at the base of another stretch of towering mountains. An enormous valley separated the camp from the checkpoint, which could barely be seen even when using binoculars. There wasn't even a village within a hundred miles. So immense in scope was the setting that I was left with a sense of ant-like insignificance.

The camp itself consisted of a couple of large vehicles, which served as sleeping quarters and cooking facility, and traditional yurts. A yurt is cylindrical in shape with a domed roof and constructed of a heavy canvas material, much like a tent. Far from appearing bland, the yurts were quite colorfully decorated and they were a matter of pride for the owners, who passed them from generation to generation. Inside, our sleeping quarters were comfortable and a stove provided heat. Since leaving Bishkek, trees were almost non-existent, so the stoves burned animal dung and coal.

After a day spent lounging around camp, the real hunting was to commence the following morning. For my guide, I drew a man about the same age as me called the "Director." He was obviously the person in charge of the operation, and his title reflected his position. We were driven several miles east to a place where a man named John and his wife lived with their two-year-old son. Apparently, this facility, which featured several metal buildings, served as another hunting camp, although I was often left guessing about the particulars due to the lack of a common language. When everyone was in the main camp, communication between us foreigners and our hosts was facilitated by a translator named Milstan. In the field, however, I just did the best I could and hoped the language barrier wouldn't be a problem at a crucial moment.

After some polite conversation, John saddled three of the resident horses, and he, I and the Director headed into the mountains. The horses were on the small side but extremely tough. Seemingly, they could go anywhere, and the guides didn't baby them one bit. The base of the mountain held snow in some locations, while in other places the ground was bare. There wasn't a tree or shrub to be found anywhere. Instead, the lowlands were dominated by tall grasses, now amber in color with the lateness of the season. These grasslands extended well onto the rolling hills that greeted us as we ascended. Beyond the closest knolls lay the mountain peaks, which were infinitely more rugged than the foothills. Naturally, as elevation was gained snow depths tended to increase.

As we rode, I began to appreciate the enormity of the country which surrounded us. The most startling discovery was just how deceiving distances could be. The smooth hills didn't look all that tall from afar, but they easily rose 1,000 feet in elevation. While riding, I would make an estimate of how long it would take to reach the top, only to find that the journey's duration would exceed my expectations by two or three times. From the crest of the foothills, the terrain steepened considerably and an additional 2,000 vertical feet of rock, snow and ice led to the closest visible peaks. Several large side valleys interrupted the mountain range at various intervals, allowing access to the interior and the opportunity to look over many more acres of sheep habitat.

It was on an excursion up one of these side valleys where I viewed my first Marco Polo ram. Actually, two rams were present: one of them had a broken horn, but the other was perfect. I wasn't any whiz at judging these unfamiliar animals; they all appeared big compared to sheep in North America. Even so, I knew I was looking at a top-end specimen. The Director, who had plenty of experience evaluating the local sheep, drew the number "63" in the snow, indicating his estimate of the ram's horn length. If that judgment was spot on, the ram would be considered a bruiser anywhere, but especially in Kyrgyzstan, where horns tended to be shorter. Unfortunately, the rams were very high on the mountain and low clouds persisted in obscuring the sheep from our sight for hours at a time. Under the circumstances, the best course of action was to wait and see if the rams would move lower. That never happened, and fading daylight forced us to retreat to camp.

The next morning, the three of us headed back to where the rams had been the previous day. We had to look around some, but we eventually found the pair in a side valley, along with about twenty other sheep and seventy ibex. For the moment, the rams were located in a spot that defied any approach to within reasonable shooting distance, so we backed out of the valley until later in the day.

We returned around 2pm, and within an hour the action started to heat up. It seemed as though the whole mountain was moving at the same time, as nearly 100 animals of all sorts began feeding. From our position below, the biggest concern was that we'd spook the ibex as we advanced towards the rams. Since they occupied the ground between us and our quarry, any ibex we disturbed could then be expected to alarm the rams, leaving us without a shot. Waiting for the ibex to drift past our line of approach burned much of the remaining daylight.

By the time we closed the distance to 500 yards it was getting dark. For some reason, my rangefinder chose this crucial moment to stop working. Even if the instrument hadn't failed mechanically, I doubted that enough light remained to obtain a decent reading of the range. Making matters worse, the circumstances were such that building a stable shooting position was nearly impossible. The rams were well above us, and I was crammed against a side hill with nothing in front of me to use as a rest. By deploying my sitting bipod in an unconventional manner, I was finally able to see the ram in the scope, but the butt of the gun rested completely on my right biceps. Instead of using my left hand to stabilize the front of the gun, it was needed at the juncture of the stock and my arm.

I was ready to take the shot, but the range was unknown and it was dark. Due to the decidedly uphill shooting angle and my weak shooting position, the only thing I knew for sure was that I was going to be hammered when I pulled the trigger. I figured the ram was at least 400 yards away, so I held on the top of ram's back to correct for the seventeen inches of expected bullet drop. When the sights looked reasonably steady, I finished my trigger squeeze. Almost immediately, stars filled my eyes and blood began running down my face. Not unexpectedly, the ram appeared to be untouched and he and his buddy could be seen slowly walking higher and farther from us. When the rams reappeared from a dip in the terrain much higher on the mountain, the Director implored me to shoot again. I figured that was a fool's errand, especially given my condition and the ridiculously long range, and refused. Foiled in our attempt, the three of us rode to John's place in the dark, where we stayed the night.

By 7am the next day, we had the rams spotted once again. We laid an ambush for them along their line of travel, but they crossed the valley much higher than we had planned for. Satisfied that they were bedded for the day, the three of us embarked on a long roundabout approach which would put us above them. Our efforts were for naught, though, as we found ourselves unable to climb the end wall of a box canyon that stood between us and the rams.

When we rode back to John's place at day's end, the fun really began! As we pulled in just before dark, it was apparent that company had arrived. Several men dressed in camouflage and speaking Russian were milling about. It didn't take long before the Director and one of the Russians were arguing with voices raised. Eventually, things quieted down and after some supper, someone arrived in a jeep to drive the Director and me back to our camp. Along the way, we stopped for a moment and the driver fired a couple of shots into the valley where we had last seen the two rams we had been pursuing.

I couldn't understand a word that had been said, nor was I ever given an explanation regarding what had transpired at John's. However, I was pretty sure we had been hunting in someone else's area, and when they arrived earlier than anticipated, we were caught on their turf. I figured the shots in the dark were an attempt to drive the rams onto the Director's side of the boundary, or to move them beyond the reach of the Russians. In any event, for the remainder of the hunt, I noticed that we never again travelled further east than that particular valley.

For late November, the temperatures hadn't been too cold to this point—30 degrees for daytime highs and slightly above zero for nighttime lows. Starting on November 23rd, things got noticeably chillier, but not painfully so. Depending upon the exact hunting location, snow depths varied from a few inches to more than two feet. We hunted to just above 13,000 feet, and generally, higher elevations featured heavier amounts of snow. No matter where snow was found its consistency was uniformly dry and granular; it was like walking in confectionary sugar.

Surprisingly, mature rams were in short supply. I had only seen two thus far, and the other hunters in camp hadn't done that well, despite covering a lot of ground and hunting from dawn to dusk each day. On November 23rd, the Director managed to find a small group of rams high above camp. We rode to their last known location, and then tracked them by foot quite a distance. We never saw them again. The day was interesting from a meteorological standpoint, however. The mountain tops were bathed in sunshine while the lower elevations were shrouded in a blanket of clouds. As we descended below 11,000 feet and into the dark soup on our ride back to camp, ice crystals began growing on my beard and mustache. Obviously, this wasn't an ordinary bank of fog.

The level of frustration over the lack of sheep was shared not only by the hunters, but by the guides also. The next day brought with it a change of tactics which illustrated just how desperate things had become. Our hosts decided to hunt as a group, using dogs and gunfire from the guides in an attempt to drive animals to waiting hunters positioned in strategic locations. For me, this approach didn't qualify as a legitimate way to hunt sheep or ibex. Frankly, I was dismayed and completely uninterested in participating. Differences in language prevented me from conveying my displeasure, though.

The first day spent using such tactics was a complete waste of time, but the second day produced some excitement. A large group of ibex was encountered by the guides low on the mountain. Shortly after the gunfire started, animals could be seen climbing towards the high mountain saddles which we hunters were guarding. One of the other hunters managed to shoot about ten times, eventually wounding one ibex, which could be seen lying next to a rock at least 1,000 yards away. Since the other hunter was nearly out of ammunition, I gave my rifle to his guide, who went below and dispatched the injured animal. The rest of us rode back to camp, arriving several hours after the sun had set.

The episode with the ibex, though distasteful in my eyes, brought into focus the difficulty in judging distance in these mountains. There hadn't been time to range the rock where the ibex were standing when the first shot was fired. After the shooting was over, my colleague asked me what I thought the range had been. My reply was 300-325 yards, which was consistent with his estimate. When he subsequently put his rangefinder on the aforementioned rock, we were both astonished to find that the actual distance turned out to be 490 yards! Armed with this knowledge, I couldn't help but revisit the shot I had taken at the Marco Polo ram. I wondered what the true distance to the ram had been, and whether I should have even pulled the trigger.

My rifle was returned around 2am, testifying to the extremely long and laborious day the guide had put in. For the remainder of the hunt, the tactics reverted to the more traditional spot-and-stalk methods, but rams weren't any easier to come by. On my final day of hunting, we actually found two groups of sheep. In the morning, we encountered a band of eight sheep, including two decent rams, in a favorable location for a stalk. The rams were busy banging heads and trying to impress the ewes, which figured to aid our approach. Nevertheless, the whole group had disappeared by the time we arrived in shooting position, spooked by wolves. In the afternoon we found a large group of lambs, ewes and rams—about ninety animals in all. Astonishingly, only one legitimate shooter was present in the entire group! Before we could even plan an approach, wolves again appeared from below and the wary sheep drifted higher into more secure terrain. The Director dropped his head and in perfect English said, "Fucking wolves."

My hunt was over. At supper on the night before my departure, I was presented with a traditional Kyrgyz wool hat called a kalpak. Shortly thereafter, I was brought to the guides' yurt, where I was shown some ibex horns. Milstan explained that the Director wanted me to take them home. Somewhat confused, I asked why I was being given another hunter's trophy. Milstan then told me that one of the guides had shot this animal for me, so that I wouldn't go home empty-handed. Summoning all the diplomatic skill at my disposal, I expressed my appreciation for the gesture, reiterated my complete satisfaction with the hunt, and politely declined on grounds that my culture frowned on the practice of claiming an animal which another person had killed.

The ride back to Bishkek was somewhat shorter in duration than the trip to the hunting area had been. The road, as before, consisted of a section of the ancient Silk Road, which traders had been using for centuries. What impressed me most were the truckers from China. Tractor trailers were headed to China with every piece of steel that the Chinese could extract from the neighboring former Soviet states. When the trucks returned, they were loaded with consumer goods. The Chinese worked as a team, and when one vehicle experienced trouble, mechanical or otherwise, it wasn't long before help arrived.

I had come an awfully long way for a prized Marco Polo ram, and although I hadn't been successful, I was still glad I had made the trip. Hunting in faraway places involved interesting and different cultures, which made for a unique experience and a chance to broaden one's horizons. The biggest impediment had been the travel, which was much more imposing than anything I had endured to that point. Nevertheless, the logistics weren't so horrible that I automatically discounted a return visit at some future time.

Perhaps the most disappointing aspect of the hunt had been the near total absence of mature rams. In Bishkek, Harv had cautioned us about not shooting the first ram we saw. We were expected to see plenty of sheep, and we were admonished to select one which was above-average. After all, killing a good ram had been billed as one of the easier elements of the hunt. The reason for the discrepancy between expectation and outcome would remain unexplained. Having seen them in person, Marco Polo sheep enjoyed a special place in my imagination, and a subsequent trip to Asia to conclude unfinished business couldn't be ruled out.

Camp at 10,000 feet. The two structures to the left are traditional yurts.

A snow-covered vista in Kyrgyzstan, where everything looks much closer than it actually is. This mountain tops out around 13,000 feet.

Another snow-covered scene higher in the rugged Tien Shan Mountains.

ROCKY MOUNTAIN BIGHORN SHEEP— 2005

My previously scheduled hunt in British Columbia was to begin my final march towards a Grand Slam® with my muzzleloader. I first had to find a new gun that was up to the task. A year before the hunt I began to research my options, not only for the gun I would choose but also for the powder and bullets that would satisfy my needs. Muzzle-loading had seen significant advances in the decade since I had taken my last sheep. In-line rifles, saboted bullets and black-powder substitutes were now common.

To this point in time, my inclination had been to avoid the newer technologies in favor of more traditional equipment. It was getting ever more difficult to maintain this stance, however, as the older products on dealer's shelves disappeared, to be replaced with more contemporary substitutes. In the end, my desire for consistency, confidence and future peace of mind regarding the availability of components overcame my ties to the past.

Practicality may have driven my shift to modern muzzle-loading, but there was one thing I steadfastly refused to compromise about: an iron-sighted aiming system. I hunted with a primitive weapon for one simple reason—it was more challenging. And in my estimation, the use of iron sights constituted the single greatest factor which contributed to the difficulty. For me, putting a fancy scope on a primitive rifle was not only historically out-of-place, but it defeated the larger purpose. Open sights limited one's effective shooting range and they were much more difficult to bring to bear on an animal than were cross hairs. That meant it was necessary to hunt harder and more skillfully to kill game, contributing to the greater sense of reward.

After much contemplation, I decided to buy a Thompson/Center Omega in .50 caliber. I replaced the factory front sight with one that allowed for more precise aiming and swapped the existing rear sight for an after-market peep sight. For components, I chose Precision Rifle's 300-grain Dead Center .44-caliber saboted bullet and Hodgdon's Triple Seven powder. From the very first shooting session, I was pleased with the performance this combination gave me. After some minor tweaking of powder weight and a lot of practice, I finally possessed what had eluded me for so long—a primitive weapon that I could completely trust.

I may have rejected the use of a scope as a means of maintaining a primitive ethic, but I wasn't a purist. If that were true, I would have hunted with a flintlock and round balls. Given my self-imposed limitations, I was still very interested in developing my capabilities to the fullest extent possible. From a ballistics standpoint, the saboted bullet I had selected was superior to the Great Plains conical I had used to kill my two previous sheep. Theoretically, that advantage would allow me to double my effective shooting range.

As a practical matter, the use of iron sights tended to negate the benefit of an aerodynamically superior bullet. When used in the conventional manner, the front bead tended to obscure the target at ranges beyond 100 yards, making precise aiming problematic. To make a long story short, by using the front bead in a unique way, I invented an aiming method which would allow me to take full advantage of my new bullet. Before long, I was capable of regularly placing my shots within the vital zone of a sheep at 200 yards.

I may have finally conquered my gun problems, but in the period leading up to the hunt I faced two significant physical ailments. While moving some plywood, I injured my right elbow. Correcting the problem would require surgery, which I scheduled after my sheep hunt. The elbow figured to be a painful inconvenience, but my other condition posed a serious threat to my ability to hunt. I had been dealing with a chronic case of plantar fasciitis in my right foot for more than a year. The chief symptom was morning pain which subsided over time. While backpacking two months prior to my hunt, things worsened considerably. Instead of my foot being sore when I got up the next morning, I couldn't even walk! Physical therapy, stretching and an injection of cortisone to the affected area eventually calmed things down, but I lost some valuable training time. Plus, as the hunt neared it still hurt to walk. I worried that the constant stress placed on the foot during the hunt would cause another major relapse, preventing me from continuing.

On September 5th I left for Cranbrook, British Columbia. Jordon Aasland met me at the airport. He and his wife Natasha owned and operated Whiteswan Lake Outfitters, situated in the East Kootenay region. The next day, Jordon and I drove to his base of operations within the hunting area. The scenery was gorgeous, and upon our arrival I was amazed to find a newly completed log lodge and two smaller log cabins. Tending to the facilities was Natasha's father Jack Rasenberg, who was visiting from Australia.

Logging was widespread in the immediate area, and the abundance of roads (active or not) provided a viable means of accessing portions of Jordon's hunting area, especially for glassing purposes. I had arrived several days prior to the official start of the hunting season in the hope that we could find some rams to hunt come opening day. Apparently, I might have some competition for the available sheep. Jordon explained that I may have been the only non-resident sheep hunter in his hunting concession, but some of the Canadians hunted sheep too, and they had the right to hunt in the same places we did.

Jordon and I spent the next couple of days checking an area where eight rams had been previously seen from one of the roads. We did some glassing from the road and we climbed into the adjoining country in an effort to more thoroughly scout the area, but we could only find two sub-legal rams. We may not have found anything worth hunting, but we did witness an once-in-a-lifetime event. From half a mile away, as we watched the rams feed, we also noticed a mountain lion carefully stalking the sheep from below. Once the lion closed to within striking distance it lunged at the closest ram. The cougar actually hooked the ram with one paw before they both disappeared into the timber. Seconds later, the ram reappeared minus the cat, which we never saw again. Claw marks on the ram's right shoulder bore witness to his narrow escape.

Having failed to find what we were looking for, we left the lodge the following morning and headed to the northernmost portion of Jordon's area. Jack chauffeured us to our departure point. From there, Jordon and I would climb 1,500 feet to the nearest campsite with full packs. After establishing a base of operations, we would hunt the surrounding country. If that didn't pan out, we would move our camp to the south, hunting as we went.

Most of the climb was inside the timber, but when we emerged into the daylight the scenery was beautiful. A large rock dome dominated the immediate foreground. Depending upon where I looked, patches of trees were still present, but they were interspersed among open sections of bare rock and vegetated hillsides. The topography consisted primarily of a long main ridge which ran roughly north to south, with short side ridges and basins emanating to the east and west. The country was also packed tightly together, which had the effect of creating a lot of very nice sheep habitat over a relatively small area. In most places the footing was relatively easy. There was still plenty of up and down, but I didn't see anything which looked particularly scary to navigate.

Jordon and I reached the campsite, set up the tent and then went looking for sheep. Over the next day and one-half, we spotted one black bear, several mule deer and a band of five rams. The sheep were located in a side valley just over the ridge from our camp. The group contained one ancient ram which had heavily broomed horns. Jordon figured the ram must have been twelve or thirteen years old, but due to his shortened horns he wasn't legal. One of his companions was younger but legal. We turned in that night satisfied with the knowledge that we were well-positioned to stalk a nearby ram come morning, opening day of the hunting season. We couldn't wait for the sun to rise, or so we thought.

Before dawn, it started snowing. When the two of us finally exited the tent at 9:30am, six inches covered the ground and we couldn't see fifty yards through the low clouds and fog. All we could do for the day was throw wood onto the fire to stay warm and keep ourselves occupied. By late afternoon it was snowing again and it snowed all night, leaving a total accumulation of twelve inches of the white stuff. Jordon said this was the most snow he had ever seen this early in the year. For a second full day, visibility was no better than it had been the day before. The next day brought mixed precipitation and continued poor glassing conditions.

Faced with a third successive day where hunting was impossible and with an uncertain outlook for the future, we decided to bail to the lodge in the hope that weather conditions further to the south were more favorable. As we packed, my disgust surfaced and I said, "I guess it just would have been too easy to climb up there and kill that ram opening day." Jordon had been thinking the same thing.

Jordon used his satellite phone to call the lodge and arrange for our transportation. Back in camp, we had a chance to eat some real food, clean up and recharge our batteries. Although the sky cleared just before dark, by the next morning the mountains were socked in once again. Jordon, Jack and I drove about in the hope that we'd find some piece of the mountain we could glass, but the low clouds thwarted our initial effort. Later in the day we made another attempt. Things had improved just enough to see the tops of the mountains.

Jordon knew his area and the local sheep herds very well. Heavy snowfall tended to cause the rams to move into certain basins, and Jordon was very interested in one particular spot. In order to visualize the area, though, it was necessary to glass from a location which was almost seven miles away. From that distance, only the spotting scope had enough magnification to spot a sheep. Almost unbelievably, through great skill and perseverance, Jordon located a group of eight rams around the corner from where the incident with the cougar had taken place. Although there was no way to determine trophy potential, weather permitting, we had sheep we could hunt the next day.

So far, my foot had been painful but I had no problems getting around, even with a heavy pack. Certainly, all the days we lost to bad weather provided a respite. That night, as we made preparations for the following day, Jordon asked if I would mind if Jack came with us. He had always wanted to be involved in a sheep hunt, but the opportunity had escaped him. I really liked Jack and I was happy to have him accompany us, as long as it was understood that he would stay behind during the final stalk, if and when that occurred.

The three of us left the lodge at 4am and drove to the log landing which would give us the best access to the area where the sheep had been the night before. Jordon's plan was to climb an adjoining ridge that would allow us to glass for the rams, and once they had been located, we could decide how to proceed. When we arrived at the landing, two unexpected events rendered the plan obsolete. First, the mountain was immersed in fog. That finding wouldn't have interfered with our attempt to reach the ridge; we'd just have to wait for the mist to lift in order to begin glassing. The second surprise really threw a monkey wrench into the works: a truck was already parked at the landing! Obviously, another hunter had seen the same sheep we had, and we were now in the unenviable position of having to compete for the rams.

Like most hunting guides, Jordon was generally a pretty easy-going guy, but he was noticeably displeased with this situation. Instead of continuing to the ridge as planned, he felt we should climb straight towards rams and hope we found ourselves closer to the sheep than the unidentified hunter when the fog lifted. This strategy wasn't without danger; we could inadvertently spook the rams in our haste, especially with limited visibility.

Snow covered the ground in most places, so as we climbed in the early morning gloom, Jordon kept track of our still-unseen competitor. We knew he was somewhere above us. Three hours into our ascent, around 9am, I heard the distinct sound of two rams banging their heads together, several hundred yards in front of us. As I stood listening, a second round of head-butting echoed back our way. Just then, the other hunter popped into view fifty yards up the slope. He was Gerry Favreau, a local hunter of note. Earlier in the hunt, Jordon had mentioned Gerry to me, describing him as "the last of the gentlemen sheep hunters."

Given the closeness of the rams, we all retreated into a small timbered gully to wait for better visibility. At first, I was relieved that a fist fight hadn't ensued. Jordon and Gerry obviously knew each other and got along well. As we visited, I was hopeful that an accommodation could be made that pleased all parties. For instance, I was willing to give up a chance at a larger ram in exchange for the first shot or an opportunity to shoot the closest legal ram. After about fifteen minutes of amiable chatter, Gerry turned to head down the mountain. He knew that Jordon hunted sheep to earn a living; he did it for fun. His final words of advice to me were, "Don't miss." Frankly, I was stunned! Gerry had affirmed the validity of Jordon's prior characterization. I was the beneficiary of his generosity and his sense of sportsmanship.

By 10:30am, the wind had cleared the mountain of low clouds and fog, allowing us to move higher. No rams could be seen from our new vantage point in a shallow saddle, despite the fact that the immediate area was all tracked up. The three of us ate lunch, and then Jordon crossed to the next ridge to try and find the missing rams. Jordon was perched on a high pinnacle, where he very carefully inched his way from place to place, carefully glassing for sheep. Eventually, he motioned for me to join him.

Grabbing my gun and some speed loaders, I started over. After approximately 300 feet of near vertical rock climbing, we were together. Jordon quietly explained that he had spotted two legal rams, and then he asked, "How comfortable are you with thirty-yard off-hand shot? At first, I thought he was kidding; nothing I had seen relative to the terrain thus far led me to believe that such a close shooting opportunity was possible. Quickly collecting myself, I was tempted to say, "Where do I sign up?" Instead, I just nodded my acceptance.

Instantly, my mind started churning as I contemplated the impending shot. The aperture of my peep sight was designed for ranges in excess of 100 yards. At a mere thirty yards, I was afraid the field of view might be too small to aim quickly, so I opted to remove the aperture and aim through its round housing. At the same time, I recognized that things could rapidly change and I might still need the aperture. So that it was immediately available, I held the aperture between my pursed lips.

I still hadn't seen the rams, which remained hidden behind the convexity of the mountain. Jordon told me to step to our right when I was ready, and shoot the ram on the right. I didn't know exactly what to expect, but I was ready to act quickly, figuring I'd only have a second or two before the sheep bolted. With the hammer cocked and the gun shouldered, I slowly eased away from the rock, looking for sheep as I stepped. The second I cleared the rock face, I saw three rams standing in a row facing me. I quickly centered the front bead in the middle of the rightmost ram's chest and fired. The three sheep whirled to our left and instantly disappeared over the top of the ridge. Jordon asked if I made a good shot. It didn't seem possible that I could have missed, so I said, "It looked good."

Five seconds later, five rams reappeared from behind the ridge and started running down in front of us. At first glimpse they all looked fine, but then I noticed that one of them didn't seem to be using its right front leg. Just then, that ram stumbled, fell and began rolling downward. A second later, the dead ram disappeared from sight over a cliff. Jordon let out a holler as I stood dumbfounded and in awe of what had just transpired. An equal mix of relief and gratitude washed over me, provoking my eyes to fill slightly. At the same moment Jordon said, "If that doesn't make you feel like crying, I don't know what will." I couldn't have been happier, but I was also more than a little anxious about the ram's condition, given its tumble off the ledge.

After handshakes, Jordon and I worked our way down to the ram. He had fallen quite some distance, coming to rest in a gully just large enough to hold him. Despite the severity of the plunge, with the exception of a broken jaw and some minor and inconspicuous tears about one hind leg and a nostril, the ram was in surprisingly good shape. Although the horns had collected a few scratches, they failed to detract from the overall impression, which was one of beauty and mass. Content with the knowledge that the ram was, in fact, dead and certain about his location, we headed back to Jack and our abandoned packs.

From his location, Jack had been able to see the whole episode unfold, and he was as excited as Jordon and me. After a group celebration and some refreshments we returned to the ram. The first order of business was an extensive photographic session. That accomplished, we caped the ram for a life-size mount. The hunt meant a lot to me, and in spite of the extra work involved, I wanted to preserve the whole trophy. By the time we finished skinning the ram and separating the edible meat it was 8pm. The trek out to the truck would be made almost completely in the dark.

Jordon carried the meat while I took the cape and horns. Jack was kind enough to carry some of my bulkier items so I'd have plenty of room for the sheep. Even so, I had at least eighty pounds on my back, and Jordon toted a hundred pounds. It took us three grueling hours to reach the truck. I lost count of the number of times I fell, especially while traversing the overgrown logging cut that served as the last real obstacle before reaching the vehicle.

Upon our arrival at the truck, Jordon held out his hand and said, "Congratulations, you're my first hunter in twenty-five years to pack out his own animal." Naturally, I took the comment as a compliment, but I honestly felt that carrying your trophy was just part of being a sheep hunter. I never deluded myself into thinking I was as tough as my guides. They always bore the heavier burden—in weight, as well as responsibility. But, I always sought to earn my guide's respect. One way of accomplishing that was to help with the heavy lifting, so to speak, give it my all and make the professional's job as easy as possible.

I may have persevered in my effort to lug the sheep out, but I was in bad shape when we finally reached the vehicle. I had incurred the usual assortment of blisters and sore muscles that an endeavor of that kind would normally produce, but I was also severely dehydrated. Since we left camp, I had only consumed one full bottle of water (32 ounces) and a few handfuls of snow. And it had been a maximum-effort day. Jordon had extra water in the truck, which was welcome, but that didn't immediately benefit me. Intravenous fluids would have helped more, but they weren't available. During the ride to the lodge I could barely hold my head up and I struggled to breathe normally.

A little past midnight we cruised into camp, twenty hours after we had departed. Natasha, her mother Pip, and Elaine the cook had waited up for us, worrying about our status. They were relieved to see us and even more excited to learn of our success. I removed my sweat-soaked clothes and huddled next to the wood stove with a blanket covering me. I couldn't immediately put any solid food on my stomach, but after sipping down three caffeinated Cokes, I was finally starting to feel better. By 2am, I had recovered significantly and even felt well enough to clean my gun before taking a well-deserved shower. A half hour later I went to bed, concluding an epic—and exhilarating—day of hunting.

I didn't sleep, but that was hardly surprising. My mind was too busy replaying the events of the day. I was up by 6am, feeling normal but famished. My foot, which had bothered me considerably while I was packing the ram, felt better than it had in weeks. Jordon and I enjoyed a relaxing recuperation day, eating to our hearts content. We even made a trip to Cranbrook to have the sheep horns inspected and plugged. The next day Gerry came to camp to visit. He brought a couple of his record-class sheep horns with him. We all had a good time talking hunting and sharing stories. We also learned that once he left us on the mountain, Gerry had gone to a suitable glassing spot so he could watch our hunt through his spotting scope.

My trip to British Columbia had been an unqualified success. My new equipment had performed well, although it must be acknowledged that the test had been pretty easy. I had overcome physical adversity and lousy weather to take the best trophy of my life—a fabulous bighorn ram with a muzzleloader. In addition to the ram, I also brought home fond memories of a great adventure, one where three other people played significant roles in the outcome. With my fifty-second birthday less than a month away, the ram and the experience made for a sensational present. Although I would forever cherish this hunt as a stand-alone event, my success signaled that, after more than ten years of struggles, I was finally back on track to fulfill a dream.

Whiteswan Lake in the foreground, with beautiful Mt. Dorman looming in the background.

This beautiful mountain scene served as the setting for two significant events: I shot my bighorn ram from the very top of the peak in the center of the picture; and the mountain lion attacked the young ram lower on the hillside.

Me and Jordon Aasland with the super bighorn ram we took in the East Kootenay region of British Columbia.

Photo by Jack Rasenberg

Jack Rasenberg, Gerry Favreau and me with my sheep horns and two of Gerry's record-class specimens.

Photo by Jordon Aasland

Desert Bighorn Sheep—2005

With my success in British Columbia, I was one step away from obtaining my coveted muzzleloader Grand Slam®. Before the hunt, I wouldn't permit myself the presumptuousness of planning for the fourth and final leg of the task. By looking too far ahead, I was sure I would jinx my bighorn hunt. And, I knew that killing a bighorn was a 50/50 proposition at best, no matter what weapon was used. However, with the bighorn now safely in the bag, I quickly turned my attention to desert sheep. In fact, I was even contemplating my options as I flew home from Canada. I kissed my wife upon my arrival, but it wasn't long before I was consumed with finding a suitable hunt in Mexico.

    The sheep-hunting season in Mexico ran roughly from November to March. My elbow surgery was scheduled for October. Under normal circumstances, I would have booked the hunt for the following year. But things didn't feel normal to me; I was plagued by a strong sense of urgency, and the prospect of waiting a full year seemed unbearable. I was also concerned that additional physical problems or changes in my eyesight could sabotage my plans. With the cooperation of my wife, I decided that I would attempt to find a hunt for the upcoming season—just months away—rather than wait. Based upon my surgeon's expectations, I figured that I'd be able to go any time after December 1st.

I attacked the problem on several fronts. I sent an email to Ivan Flores, the owner of the ranches where I had hunted previously, in order to explore the possibilities of a hunt, but I didn't receive a response. I reviewed past and current editions of Wild Sheep and Grand Slam/Ovis magazines for reports regarding desert sheep hunts. I also checked out the advertisements in both magazines placed by outfitters who conducted sheep hunts in Mexico. While searching, I came across an ad for Sierra Grande Outfitters, based in Colorado. A phone number in the States and the likelihood of dealing with someone who spoke English seemed a good place to start, so I gave owner Les Ezell a call.

As we spoke, two things quickly became apparent: Les could accommodate my desire to hunt during the upcoming season and the setting for the hunt would be the same ranches I had hunted the first time I travelled to Mexico. As Les related details of the hunt, I recognized most of the names and places. Obviously, he and Ivan Flores had a business relationship. I hadn't anticipated such serendipity when I picked up the phone, but I was pleased to be headed somewhere familiar, especially as it related to those who would guide me. I liked and respected Martín and Jorge. In short order, Les and I formalized the arrangements for a mid-December hunt.

The settled-upon hunting dates threatened to interrupt my deer-hunting season, but that was a price I was willing to pay for the privilege of taking a desert bighorn. As things turned out, by the time I left for Mexico, I had already killed a couple of nice bucks. In fact, I had taken one of them less than twenty-four hours before I headed to the airport. Due to my impending trip, I hadn't even planned on hunting that day, but I couldn't resist the twelve inches of fresh tracking snow that unexpectedly fell during the night. The flight to Phoenix was as peaceful and relaxed as any I had ever experienced, as I rested from the exertions of the previous day and the hectic, last-minute preparations for the trip to Mexico. As I sat in the plane with my eyes closed, I just kept replaying the details of my successful deer hunt, all the while hoping that I would be as fortunate in the desert.

I met up with Les in Phoenix while we waited to board our final flight to Hermosillo. Ivan greeted us as we exited the plane. Gratefully, my luggage arrived with me. After clearing Mexican Customs, we first headed to a local shooting range, where Ivan insisted that I shoot my gun using the powder he had obtained at my request. I usually didn't bother to confirm my muzzleloader's zero. Maybe the only advantage to using iron sights was their simplicity. Unlike scopes, which had internal adjustments, I could examine my sights and determine whether or not they were set precisely as they had been before I turned the gun over to the airlines. Assuming nothing was amiss, I normally elected not to shoot the gun, which only served to deplete the limited supply of components I had on hand. Besides, I could never just shoot a black-powder gun; I also had to clean it, which was time-consuming. On this occasion, however, I chose to humor Ivan.

After firing a single shot at the range we were back in the car for the final leg of our journey. We pulled into the Pico Johnson ranch, the setting where I killed my first desert bighorn, late in the afternoon. Since my last visit a few improvements had been made, including a new ranch house. It was nice to see Jorge and Martín again; there were some new faces, also. After supper, Ivan headed back to Hermosillo and the rest of us hit the sack.

We rose early and drove to a good spot from which we could glass for sheep. By 8am, Jorge had found a really nice ram high on the mountain to our front. This particular unnamed mountain was distinct from Pico Johnson proper, which loomed to our left. The mountain the solitary ram called home lacked the height and formidableness of the named peak, but it still appeared challenging. As we watched the feeding ram, it soon became apparent that he was singularly cautious. The ram routinely took a step, stopped and then looked around before putting his head down. He repeated this sequence time after time as he advanced, and only rarely did the ram take more than a single step. Because of this behavior, I began referring to the ram as "Old One-step."

When our wary adversary finally bedded for the day, we ducked out of sight and moved towards him. In the full sunshine and warming temperatures, it didn't take long to start sweating. The lousy footing didn't help either. For the most part, the mountain consisted of rotten sandstone, which tended to give way just as I transferred weight from one foot to the other. Eventually, Martín, Jorge, Les and I reached the top, some 300 yards down the ridgeline from the resting ram. Unbeknownst to me, the backside of the mountain contained sheer drop-offs, limiting our ability to maneuver out of the ram's sight.

We needed to gain at least another 100 yards before I would consider shooting, so Martín and I dropped our packs and moved forward alone in an effort to minimize the chance of being detected by the ram's keen eyesight, as well as to reduce the noise we might make. In one place, the two of us crossed through a section that didn't offer much cover. Nevertheless, we escaped notice by proceeding one at a time and by waiting for the ram's attention to be elsewhere. To our surprise, further down the ridge, we saw a bunch of other sheep below us on the side of the spine facing the Sea of Cortez. The group contained some rams, but for the time being, they weren't a priority.

Martín and I finally ran out of real estate and could advance no further. The rangefinder told us the still-bedded One-step was 200 yards away. That happened to be the upper limit of my shooting range, but at least the ram was level with us and wind wasn't a factor. Working against me was the awkward shooting position I was left to deal with. I was positioned against a vertical wall, trying to keep myself from slipping by digging my toes into the stubborn sandstone. I was neither standing nor sitting, but instead, I assumed a crouched posture. The gun was comfortably resting on a ledge in the rock.

The ram was facing us in his bed. As we waited for him to stand, I continually worked to solidify my stance by scraping depressions in the rock for my feet and elbows. Before long, I had improved my shooting platform considerably. The problem was that my betterments only allowed for a narrow shooting window. If I couldn't shoot at the ram while he remained within a few steps of his bed, I wouldn't have enough stability to shoot at all. In addition, I couldn't wait all day in the awkward position I had been forced into. If the ram didn't get up fairly soon, muscle tremors, begotten by fatigue, could destroy the steadiness I had worked so hard to create.

Fortunately, my prayers for events to move quickly were answered—kind of. Within ten minutes the ram stood, but he was still facing us, offering me no immediate shot. Next, for the first time all day, instead of taking a single step, Old One-step took several. He was now broadside, but slightly outside of my constrained shooting window. It took a few seconds to make the necessary adjustments and bring the gun to bear. I applied the proper sight picture for the distance and finished my trigger pull. Just as the gun discharged, the ram took a step down off his pedestal.

The hold may have been slightly too far back but it was perfect for elevation. At first, I thought the ram's rapid disappearance from view could be attributed to the bullet striking the spine. What I failed to consider, at least for the moment, was the bullet's time of flight. Upon leaving the barrel, the bullet would consume one-half of a second to reach a target 200 yards distant. Compared to a center-fire rifle, that's pretty slow. By the time the bullet reached the ram, he had dropped out of our sight, and the slug sailed harmlessly over his back. Whatever the explanation, it was evident that the bullet had missed its mark as soon as we observed an unharmed ram cautiously climbing higher in the rocks on the other side of the depression which had momentarily hidden him from our view.

One-step was out of reach, but I had reloaded my gun and we still had an opportunity to check out the sheep we had encountered during our stalk. As Martín and I retraced our steps, we soon noticed seven or eight sheep bunched together on a promontory about 100 yards away and slightly below us. When Martín looked through his binoculars, he noticed a respectable ram standing at the far right of the group. The ram wasn't as big horn-wise as the ram which had brought us to this high place, but that hardly mattered to me. I had put up with my share of bad luck while hunting over the years, and while I didn't feel entitled to good fortune, neither was I willing to spit in the face of hunting gods bearing gifts.

This time, my shooting platform would be more conventional. I assumed a prone position with my head lower than my body. Once the sights looked good, I cocked the hammer of the Omega and sent the last round at my immediate disposal towards the ram. He reacted as though he was hit, but he didn't move much. Martín could see the ram coughing blood as he watched through his binoculars, suggesting the bullet had penetrated the lungs. After a few minutes, the entire group of sheep began moving around. The wounded ram worked his way to the edge of the cliff, shivered and then did a backflip to the rocks thirty feet below. Just like that, my quest was over!

Les and Jorge knew something had been going on, but they couldn't see the sheep from their position. After the missed shot on One-step, which they had witnessed, we used hand signals to inform them of our intentions. With another shot fired and the ram now dead, Martín and I met Les and Jorge in a nearby saddle, where we all exchanged handshakes before descending to the ram. We didn't have far to go, but the terrain was nearly vertical. All the while, I kept my fingers crossed, hoping that the ram wouldn't be all busted up from the fall.

The ram had taken some hits, but all the important pieces were intact. Patches of hair were missing, but not about the face, neck and shoulders. Horn material had been gouged from the underside of one horn, but the damage was superficial and inconspicuous, and the horns hadn't been broken. Relieved that the ram had satisfactorily survived his dive off the cliff, I turned my attention to the cause of his death. Upon examination, it appeared that only one lung had been hit, which was consistent with the ram's post-shot behavior. The downhill shooting angle and the ram's presentation were contributing factors, but I bore most of the blame for both lungs not being impacted, as bullet placement had been higher than I wanted.

The customary round of posing for pictures was the next order of business, followed closely by trophy preservation and meat retrieval. With four strong people present, we divided the sheep so that no one's pack was unduly heavy for the trek back down to the road. The footing was no better than it had been for the climb up to this place, but we arrived safely at the truck around 4pm, sweaty and tired. Back at the ranch house, a late lunch, showers, dinner and a final round of celebrations capped a memorable day.

Everyone but the ranch hands left for Hermosillo early the next morning. The first stop was Ivan's office. He informed me that the permits which would allow me to transport my ram back into the States wouldn't be ready any time soon. I would have to wait for my trophy to be shipped to me, which was not my preference. Looking at the bright side, the delay would make for a speedier visit with the people in U.S. Customs. Les and I spent the rest of the day together before meeting Ivan for supper. The next day I left for home, arriving just past midnight after a tiring day of travel. Just that quickly, my excursion to Mexico was over.

The hunt had been everything I had hoped it would be—successful and short. When I left home, my only objective was to kill a ram and get back as quickly as possible. I was focused very narrowly on completing my longstanding goal and little else. In fact, after my bighorn hunt in September, an anticlimactic air hung over the whole desert sheep hunt. I regretted this feeling, but I just wasn't capable of viewing the experience in any other context. I expected to get a sheep; I just didn't know how long it would take. Certainly, the briefness of the hunt itself and the role that blind luck had played in its outcome did little to alter my perspective. I didn't work very hard; I didn't struggle very long; and I wasn't forced to rely on skill very much—but I was very happy that I had succeeded.

The setting of goals is an interesting contrivance, unique to humans. Goals serve to motivate, inspire and provide purpose to our lives. Of course, goal-setting has its dark side: obsession and the reliance on illegal or unethical methods. By confining myself to a primitive weapon and the use of iron sights, I had set the bar higher than most people would have dared, which made this Grand Slam® particularly rewarding. Sure, I spent some of my kid's inheritance along the way, but I hadn't crossed any boundaries of behavior which would serve to diminish the achievement or give me reason for regret. This particular goal had taken me more than twelve years to realize, and I was extremely proud of its accomplishment. I was also humbled by my good fortune and grateful to all those who helped make it possible.

When I returned from Mexico, I immediately gathered the materials to document both of my slams before submitting the required paperwork to Grand Slam/Ovis. I was assigned Grand Slam® #1288 and my second slam was recognized as Muzzleloader Slam #5. All four of the sheep taken with the black-powder gun qualified for inclusion and were entered into the *Longhunter Society*, the Muzzleloading Big Game Record Book. As far as my research could determine, I'm the only person to have taken a Grand Slam® of sheep with an iron-sighted muzzleloader!

This desert sheep completed my second Grand Slam and my first with a muzzleloader.

Photo by Les Ezell

Jorge rests beneath the cliff my ram took a dive from.

Dall Sheep—2007

Now what? That was the question I faced in the wake of my muzzleloader slam. My preoccupation with one major goal had precluded the consideration of any future hunting plans. For the first time in years I had no direction, but the interruption gave me an opportunity to thoroughly evaluate myself and my desires. Initially, all I had were questions: Did I still want to hunt sheep? Was I still capable of hunting sheep? Did I want to hunt in North America or elsewhere? What about hunting animals other than sheep? What role would my muzzleloader play in my hunting future?

As I sifted through the underlying issues at the root of these questions, I began to develop some clarity of purpose. Sheep still excited me in ways other animals didn't, and the mountains continued to hold a special allure. While it was true that I was no longer a young man, I felt that I was in my sheep-hunting prime, physically. Consequently, I came to the realization that I wanted to hunt sheep as long as I was able. I gave serious consideration to hunting sheep and/or goats outside of North America, but I hated the travel and very few of the potential overseas destinations were easy to reach. Although I didn't forever rule out hunting elsewhere in the world, for the near term, I decided to stick to my native continent. There were plenty of mountain ranges and places in North America I hadn't yet laid eyes on and I really liked hunting with my new equipment, so I finally settled on obtaining a second Grand Slam® with my muzzleloader as my next great hunting objective.

Due to the fact that I had doubled up on hunts in 2005, I intentionally chose not to hunt in 2006. Dall sheep often comprised a starting point for sheep hunters, whether they were first-timers or people like me. As I thought about where I'd like to go to hunt the white sheep, Steve Johnson's name came immediately to mind. Steve had been my guide years before when I hunted in the Wrangells. We had stayed in touch, and he now operated his own hunting company, Ultimate Alaskan Adventures. Steve had been trying to cajole me into hunting with him for a while, and the time now seemed right. I called and we quickly settled on hunting dates for the 2007 season.

Steve had me apply for a sheep tag in some of Alaska's premier limited-draw areas. If I was fortunate enough to be drawn, that's where we'd hunt; if not, we'd be hunting the Tonsina walk-in area of the Chugach Mountains. My name didn't come up in the lottery, so the Chugach became the setting for the hunt. Steve was able to accommodate my desire to maximize my hunting days. We'd slip into the hunting area a few days before the season opened on August 10th. Hopefully, that would allow us to locate some rams and be in good position come opening day.

I left for Alaska on August 5th. Problems with planes caused me to arrive in Anchorage four hours later than scheduled. Nonetheless, Steve was there to meet me at 2:30am local time. I felt as though I had been pulled through a knot hole backwards as we drove to Steve's house in Eagle River. After an abbreviated night of sleep, I met Steve's wife Emily before we started assembling our gear for the ride to the hunting area. By 1pm we were on the road, and five hours later we arrived at our starting point for the hunt—a pull-off along the Richardson Highway.

We shouldered our packs in a light drizzle and began our trek. Steve explained that it would take about five hours of climbing to make our way into the high alpine country the sheep called home. Using the convenience of a brook, which served as a highway through the brush, the two of us climbed for a couple of hours before setting up camp for the night. The remainder of the journey would wait until morning. Unfortunately, the going would prove to be much tougher for the first half of the second day, as we were forced to deviate from the waterway. Instead of stepping around rocks in the streambed, we had to struggle through boulder-strewn dry creek beds and thick alders. Finally, though, we popped into the open and enjoyed some easier walking. All the while, the mosquitoes had been horrible; they would remain so for the duration of the hunt.

It was nice to be clear of the brush, but Steve and I still had more climbing ahead of us. We kept walking, occasionally stopping to glass as we proceeded. Our early attempts failed to find any sheep, though. Around 3pm, we found a good campsite and set up the tent. For the rest of the day Steve and I accessed some nearby lookouts in an effort to locate our quarry, but we came up empty.

Now that Steve and I had gained some elevation and we were clear of the brush, I could better appreciate the lay of the land. Basically, we were headed towards a long ridge which ran towards the Copper River to our south. A couple of unconnected mountains stood between us and the ridge, which consisted of a series of peaks separated by saddles. The saw-tooth undulations varied in width and steepness. Valleys paralleled the ridge on both sides. The bottoms contained very little brush, and the low vegetation that emanated from the moist valley floors petered out about half way up the adjoining side slopes. Although snow only existed in distinct pockets where we were, the high country across the valley to our west contained pocket glaciers and snow-capped peaks. The ridge to the east was gentler than the one we occupied, and the white tops of Mt. Wrangell, Mt. Sanford and Mt. Blackburn could be seen in the distance. The landscape was rugged, but not as unforgiving as that encountered on my last visit to the Chugach Mountains.

On August 8th, our second full day of hiking, Steve and I covered a lot of ground, including a fair amount of climbing. We stopped to glass on occasion, but despite our best efforts, we still hadn't seen a sheep or much in the way of sheep sign. Later in the afternoon, we reached a large flat plain situated between mountains and made camp. The scenery was as dramatic as the bugs were unrelenting. That evening, we endured a two-hour thunderstorm from the confines of the tent.

Low clouds and fog from the previous night's storm persisted into the next day. To access the long ridge, we first had to climb about 1,800 feet. Assuming the weather was about to improve, Steve and I started up. By the time we approached the very top, a light mist had turned to a heavy rain. With no suitable place available to erect the tent, we were forced to retreat a couple of hundred feet down the mountain to a flat bench, where we hastily set up the tent and scurried in to escape the downpour. It's a good thing we did, too. The entire day was miserable; it even slushed for a while. Once the storm stopped around 8pm, we were treated to the sight of a beautiful rainbow across the valley, just before the sun set. Our late-day glassing efforts failed to find a single sheep.

This hunt was entirely self-supported, which meant that Steve and I were carrying everything we would need for the duration. There were no cabins or food caches, and no one would be re-supplying us from the air. As a result, our packs were heavy from the start and we were completely reliant on each other. Steve had a satellite phone in the event of a true emergency, but other than that, we were on our own. As the days ticked by and the miles began to add up, I began to appreciate that should I kill a sheep, the return trip to the truck was likely to be brutal, given the added weight of the animal and the distance we would be forced to cover.

From our high vantage point, August 10th dawned clear and dry, portending a stretch of more stable weather. Steve and I started down the ridge in search of sheep. We'd alternately climb, glass, descend to the next saddle and then glass some more. The sequence was repeated until the hour grew late, whereupon we stopped in a suitable location and set up the two-man tent. For the first time, though, we had some encouraging news on the sheep-finding front. I saw some lambs and ewes across the valley in the morning, and Steve spotted four sub-legal rams on the next peak down the ridge. Late in the day, I saw two rams well down the ridge. They were too far away to evaluate and they quickly disappeared from view, but they were heading our way. As we turned in for the night, Steve and I both felt optimistic about the coming day.

From our glassing spot early the next morning, Steve managed to find the four small rams from the day before, as well as a new group of five rams. The second band was moving rapidly in our direction, making it impossible to judge the trophy potential of any of its members. Where they had come from we didn't know, but it appeared as though the rams would pass through a notch in the mountain well below the two of us. We quickly descended 200 yards in order to be in position to shoot. Of course, our prospects depended on the rams continuing along their expected path and a legal ram being among the bunch.

We waited at our chosen ambush point for some time, but no sheep showed. Obviously, they had taken a different course, but where had they gone? Not that long ago, nine separate rams in two different groups were visible. Now, nary a sheep could be seen. Steve and I took a break to consider our next move. We didn't care about the four immature rams, but we still didn't know whether the group of five contained any possible shooters. We had to find them before we continued our journey further down the ridge.

Steve thought the best course of action was to climb to the nearest peak so we could survey most of the surrounding real estate. He didn't expect to immediately be in a shooting situation, so we dropped our packs. Steve did suggest I bring my gun and rangefinder, just in case. As we neared the top, we noticed fresh tracks in a patch of snow. It was impossible to tell whether the tracks belonged to the sheep we were seeking, but their discovery gave us hope. As the two of us carefully advanced down a side ridge emanating from the main spine, Steve suddenly stopped. He had white below him, and this time it wasn't snow.

As we hid behind a rock outcropping, Steve peeked below with his binoculars and then flashed me his full hand, indicating five sheep were present. We had found the missing group of five rams. Apparently, they made a U-turn when out of our sight earlier in the day. The sheep were over 200 yards away, and Steve still couldn't see enough of them to determine their legality. Down the ridge, a large boulder sat at the transition point where the slope steepened considerably. If we could make our way there, not only would we have cover, but we'd be able to judge trophy quality and I'd be within muzzleloader range.

The wind was in our face and the sound of running water from a creek in the valley floor promised to drown out some of the noise we could be expected to make. Still, the route we needed to take was littered with loose shale. The footing could be likened to walking downhill on small plates of china, making a completely silent approach impossible. By crouching low, the boulder provided just enough cover to mask our movement. By taking our time, we managed to slide in behind the boulder without being seen or heard.

When Steve peered down this time, he had an unobstructed view of the rams, which were lying peaceably in their beds. Best of all, two of the rams were shooters. One ram had heavier bases and broomed horns, while the other legal ram was well past full curl and still had his lamb tips. I snuck a peek from my side of the boulder, and deploying my rangefinder, I discovered the rams were 150 yards away at a thirty degree shooting angle.

I wouldn't have a shot until the rams stood, and given the hour of the day and the rams' disposition, it looked like that might not happen for some time. Being forced to wait for an extended period before shooting was an exercise in mental and emotional discipline. With the objective so tantalizingly close physically, yet still out of reach temporally, the mind tended to lose focus. Worse still, the devilish subconscious had time to erode confidence by sowing seeds of doubt born of previous failures. At the same time, the pressure to perform threatened to become more acute with each passing minute.

Earlier in my hunting career I had been in similar situations, but I lacked the means to cope as effectively as I would have liked. At this stage of my life, I still didn't relish the position I found myself in, but I was better prepared to deal with the scenario I faced. I concentrated on controlling my heart rate by consciously regulating my breathing. I repeatedly visualized the expected series of events leading up to and through the gun discharging, making sure to picture a dead sheep as the eventual outcome in every instance. The impending shot was well within my capabilities, so most importantly, I constantly reminded myself of that fact. This exercise served a dual purpose: it provided positive reinforcement; and it helped prevent the unfamiliar aspects of the situation, such as the steep shooting angle and the wide-open panorama, from making the shot seem more difficult than it really was.

As we waited, Steve and I also debated which ram we should kill. In the end, the choice was really a toss-up, but given the opportunity, consensus seemed to favor the broomed ram. As time behind the boulder dragged on, though, I said, "I might just shoot the first one to stand up." Finally, after more than an hour of waiting, the full-curl ram stood. The circumstances allowed for a practice run, so I decided to take aim at him using the top of the boulder to steady the gun. I placed the front bead in the proper relation to the ram's body and the sights were incredibly stable. I raised my cheek from the stock, resigned to wait for the broomed ram to get up, but I immediately reconsidered. The steady sight picture on the broadside ram proved too tempting. For the moment, a perfect opportunity existed; the future was up for grabs.

I quickly refocused on the sights and when I was satisfied with their placement and steadiness, I finished my trigger pull. The gun roared, and all five rams began running. Assuming I had missed, I started cursing at myself. Steve urged me to reload, but he didn't realize what I had known all along—this was a one-shot proposition! I had no components at hand for a follow-up shot. It was just then that I noticed the ram stumble, prompting me to grab Steve's binoculars. The ram was clearly struggling and blood could be seen on his flank, centered about the heart and lungs. In the space of seconds, the ram was dead and my premature self-disgust was replaced by elation.

I had my ram, but the action wasn't yet over. The broomed ram and one of his smaller subordinates were cautiously climbing towards Steve and me, unaware of our location. The duo kept coming until they reached a position above us where we were no longer hidden from their view.

Incredibly, the big ram stopped a mere twelve feet away! It was an impressive sight to have the old broomed ram standing so close, staring at us. I'll never forget his flaring nostrils and statuesque appearance against the rugged backdrop, perfectly lit by the late afternoon sun. After a few special moments, the two rams bounded out of sight.

Steve and I now had an opportunity to celebrate our success and the extra treat we had been afforded. We climbed back to our packs before making our way down to the fallen ram. He was an extremely pretty animal. His horns had good length and mass, and near perfect symmetry. The curl was somewhat tight and the horns tipped well out to the sides. Despite my initial doubts regarding the shot, which had been based solely on the ram's reaction, the bullet had been perfectly placed. I couldn't have been happier with the ram or my execution.

It's a truism in hunting that the real work starts once an animal is down. In this particular case, I was about to experience an extreme example of that adage. The ram was taken about 3:30pm. By the time we took pictures, attended to the sheep and loaded our packs, a couple of hours had passed. Getting down off a mountain with heavy loads is always one of the toughest—and most dangerous—aspects of sheep hunting. Sheep rarely die in easy-to-access spots. Precipitous footing and steep terrain made this down-climb especially nerve-racking. Nonetheless, we arrived at the valley floor at 8pm, whereupon we made camp and ate supper. I also boiled some water and cleaned the gun before calling it a night.

Steve and I slept well, rising early to start our long march back to the truck. There was no possibility that the journey could be made in a single day. Hopefully, the trip's duration wouldn't exceed two days. Steve toted more weight than me, but with the addition of the ram's head, horns and cape, my pack tipped the scales at eighty pounds.

We walked steadily for most of the day, stopping to rest and eat from time to time. The high clouds, moderate temperatures and lack of rain made for good going. Late in the day we faced a serious ordeal—a climb totaling 1,200 feet. The weight we were carrying, combined with our depleted condition, transformed the effort into a torture test. When we finally reached the top, we made camp for the night.

August 13th dawned sunny, hot and humid. Fortunately, the bulk of the trip, both in time and exertion, was behind us. Even though most of what remained of the trek was downhill, we still had to battle the dry creek beds and the choking alders. Steve and I were quickly soaked with sweat from our efforts. During the descent, I drank over three liters of water, which didn't begin to replace what I had lost through perspiration. After five additional grueling hours we finally reached the truck—exhausted, bug-bitten, sore and blistered.

Steve and I stopped twice during the drive back to Eagle River. First, we ate a well-deserved meal in Copper Center. Greasy cheeseburgers and fries were the order of the day, as we attempted to recoup the pounds we had shed during the hunt. Before touching my food, I visited the rest room to clean up a bit. When I looked in the mirror, the grungiest person I ever saw was staring back. The second stop was in Glennallen, where we presented the sheep to the Fish and Wildlife people for inspection. We pulled into Steve's about 7pm, happy to be back to civilization.

Before I left for home, Steve used the topographical software on his computer to chart our long haul back to the truck. An electronic pencil mapped the route we had taken and the software calculated the distance at an honest fifteen miles. That's a very long way when carrying that much weight in such tough country, especially for someone who was approaching his fifty-fourth birthday. The fact was: I wouldn't have survived this hunt twenty years earlier. I could be satisfied with the knowledge that my physical preparation was paying dividends.

I was rightfully pleased with all aspects of my performance, and tickled with the ram we were fortunate enough to kill. Even so, I needed a week of relative inactivity to recover from my exertions. I came to the conclusion that I wouldn't want to take on a hunt of this severity again. However, I'll always cherish the agony and the ecstasy of the Tonsina walk-in area. For those who believe in fair-chase hunting, there are very few hunts which could rival this experience.

One of our camping sites in the Tonsina walk-in area. You just can't beat the views.

Guide Steve Johnson (l) and me with the pretty Dall ram we took in the Chugach Mountains of Alaska.

Photo by Steve Johnson

All loaded up and ready to head back to the road, which was fifteen miles away. I'm carrying 80 pounds of sheep and equipment.

Photo by Steve Johnson

Our last camp. After walking for nine hours, a 1,200-foot climb brought us to this spot, tired but happy that most of the work was behind us.

Photo by Steve Johnson

ROCKY MOUNTAIN BIGHORN SHEEP—2008

At the conclusion of my 2005 bighorn hunt with Jordon and Natasha Aasland, I asked them if it was possible to return the following summer, just to visit and enjoy the majesty of the setting. I really wanted my wife to experience the beauty of British Columbia, and I knew the Whiteswan Lake facilities would impress her. I offered to help Jordon with the myriad of chores an outfitter must take care of when preparing for the upcoming hunting season. Jordon and Natasha graciously agreed to have us as guests.

The four of us spent quite a bit of time together at the Safari Club International convention that winter, prior to our upcoming visit in July of 2006. Janet and I subsequently enjoyed our week in British Columbia, and before we left, I approached Jordon about a future bighorn hunt. In response he said, "Why would you want to do that again?" His comment took me a little off guard, but I thought I understood his less-than-enthusiastic reply. Our first hunt together had been special on many levels. The likelihood of a repeat performance wasn't good, and an unsuccessful second hunt might detract from the first. From my perspective, nothing could ever diminish what we had achieved the first time around, so I said, "We can't possibly top what we did last time, we can only add to it." A second grab at the brass ring was arranged for October 2008.

Janet and I returned to British Columbia in the summer of 2007 to spend time with the Aaslands, enjoy the mountains and assist in a cabin-building project. The Safari Club conventions provided additional opportunities for the four of us to touch base. As my hunt approached, I knew two things would be different this time: Janet would be accompanying me, and I would be able to share at least some of the experience with her; and Jordon and I would hunt as friends.

On September 30th, Janet and I left home for Cranbrook, arriving later in the day without incident. The next morning, we headed to Whiteswan Lake, along with four goat and elk-hunting clients of the Aaslands. The cabin which Janet and I helped build the previous summer served as our sleeping quarters. Once we settled in, I began organizing my gear for the impending hunt. To start, Jordon wanted to check out the area at the far north of his concession, where we had all the snow in 2005. He hadn't taken a ram from that location in four years, which increased our chances of finding some mature animals.

Jordon and I left the lodge at 6am the next morning, driving as far as the available logging road would allow. By 8:15am, we were climbing the familiar path to our old campsite. The day was a bit too warm for the level of exertion required, but we made good time. Once the camp was satisfactorily set up, we lightened our loads and went looking for sheep. Just before dark, I spotted five rams in the basin below our camp. I'm sure Jordon was astonished by my glassing prowess. On the first hunt, every sheep I saw had to be pointed out to me.

The impending darkness had prevented a thorough evaluation of the rams' trophy potential the previous afternoon, but that was the first order of business for the new day. Jordon looked long and hard, but no matter which angle the rams were viewed from, none of them were legal. Besides the five sheep, the basin was also home to five young mule deer. Both species kept us entertained for much of the day. Later in the afternoon, while glassing with his binoculars, Jordon saw what he thought was a bleached out sheep skull sitting on a rock pile half a mile away. Convinced that his eyes hadn't betrayed him, Jordon descended to the heap of rocks, retrieved the skull and found both of the loose horns nearby. The ram had most likely died during the previous winter. The horns had good mass and the tips were heavily broomed. The remains now serve as an item of curiosity at the lodge.

The next two days featured deteriorating weather conditions. Jordon and I went looking for legal rams to hunt the first day, but came up empty. Rain and low clouds made glassing difficult. It rained for most of that night, and by dawn the wind was blowing thirty miles per hour and it was snowing. We both felt like we'd witnessed this same show from this exact location before. With no legal rams at hand and faced with the prospect of impossible hunting conditions, we decided to bail before things got really nasty. We retreated to the lodge, where we had a chance to shower and dry our wet gear, not to mention visit with our wives.

Early on October 6th, Jordon and I headed by truck to glass for sheep from some of Jordon's preferred lookouts. The air was cold but the sky was clear. Significant snow covered the high country. While looking into the Mutton Creek area, we observed four rams plowing through deep snow at the top of the ridge before descending into the drainage. The rams were five miles away, so it wasn't possible to evaluate any of them for horn size. After lunch, we concentrated on the area where I had killed my ram in 2005. I don't know how he did it, but Jordon found four more rams bedded in the timber low on the mountain. There wasn't any snow on the ground to provide contrast, either. Jordon was once again glassing with his spotting scope, and he managed to identify what he thought was a piece of horn amongst the trees. Through remarkable talent and sheer persistence, that little bit of horn eventually materialized into four rams!

Based upon their respective locations, Jordon figured that the Mutton Creek rams would be more accessible than the second group, so we left the lodge at 4:30am the next morning in an attempt to be in position to catch the rams while they were still up and feeding. Once we parked the truck, we walked uphill along an old logging road in the dark for about five miles to reach another of Jordon's campsites. Fifteen minutes after we arrived, around 9:30am, Jordon had the four rams in his spotting scope. From our vantage point one of the rams looked pretty good, but we'd have to get closer to make a final determination.

There was a mountain between us and the rams which would afford us the view we sought, so the two of us immediately set off to scale that peak. From the top, we had an unobstructed view of the rams from above, plus the timbered ridge we occupied offered us cover. As Jordon looked over the sheep from our hideout, it was clear that one of the rams was legal. Besides his impressive horns, the ram was also noteworthy for his deep chocolate-brown coloration. Jordon was even able to take some excellent photographs of the ram through the spotting scope as he went about his business.

As Jordon and I continued to keep an eye on the sheep, we had some weather-related issues to deal with. The wind was blowing strongly from the start, making for a cold sit, but then a storm blew in. Before we knew it, we were enveloped in thunder, lightning, rain, hail and finally snow. Many of the nearby spruce trees were dead but standing, and as they swayed with the wind, I couldn't determine if a lightning strike or a falling tree posed the greater threat to our safety.

Finally, the storm moved out and, once again, we only had to deal with the wind and cold. A good thing about hunting bighorns is that it's usually possible to start a fire.

The ever-present timber serves as a source of fuel not found when hunting the high alpine of Alaska, for instance. To spell the cold, it's usually a simple matter to duck into some inconspicuous place, start a fire and keep warm without sacrificing the hunt. In our case, we simply retreated several yards down the backside of the ridge. As one of us fed the fire and warmed himself, the other kept an eye on the rams. On this day, the combustion of dead limbs certainly made our vigil more tolerable.

After waiting most of the day, Jordon decided to make an attempt at the rams. By then, they had moved out of sight and we didn't know their exact location. Jordon suspected they might be feeding in a bowl which bordered the place where we had seen them last. To reach the rams, we first had to descend from our lookout and then make another significant climb—our third of the day. Once we occupied the same mountain the sheep were on, we could work our way down the ridge, looking for sheep as we progressed. Snow covered the ground, so we could also look for tracks to help us zero in on the rams' location.

Jordon and I managed to reposition ourselves without incident, but we still faced some obstacles. The day was getting late and the temperature had dropped below freezing. That made for increasingly noisy walking as the half foot of snow started to crust over. Our footing also suffered from the effects of the falling mercury. As we advanced down the ridgeline we encountered no sheep, nor were there tracks present to lead us to the rams' hiding place. With the odds of inadvertently spooking the rams greater than those for a successful blind stalk, we decided to back out of the area and descend to camp. The rams were undisturbed and they'd be somewhere nearby in the morning.

Jordon easily found the rams the next morning. They were feeding lower on the mountain, near a series of waterfalls along a small creek. We started directly up the drainage towards them, being careful to stay out of sight. The wind was unreliable, though. On a couple of occasions the breeze swapped directions. Even though we were still a long way from the sheep, they could be seen with their noises in the air, evaluating what we supposed was a few molecules of our scent.

The two of us finally advanced to a point where we entered a large block of timber. This allowed us better concealment and more latitude regarding our route to the sheep. We swung to our left until we reached the top of the timber, which put us roughly at the same elevation as the rams. Shedding our packs and taking only essential items, we slowly made our way towards the place where we had last seen the sheep, more than an hour earlier. At one point Jordon said, "We're either going to kill that ram or they'll be gone." As I surveyed the landscape, it was becoming apparent to me that should the rams still be there, any shot I might have wouldn't be a long one.

As Jordon and I slowly inched forward, we approached the last roll of topography which prevented a view of the creek bottom. We were both looking intently at all the visible real estate for any sign of a sheep. When Jordon peeked over the crest of the hill, the first thing he saw was a ram bedded just above the waterway, on the opposite side of the creek. He happened to be the lone legal ram; he was completely unaware of our presence; and he was just 75 yards away!

The two of us had a large rock for cover, so I immediately began maneuvering for the most stable shooting position I could find. I was reluctant to shoot until the ram stood, giving me full access to his vitals and the greatest possible margin for error. We hadn't been in place for five minutes when the wind shifted. We both felt the errant breeze; at the same instant, all the rams stood and looked our way. Jordon immediately whispered, "We're busted!" I didn't need any prodding. In fact, before Jordon completed his remark, using the rock for a rest, I was already fine-tuning my aim on the chest of the ram, which was standing broadside. A split second later the gun bellowed.

Jordon exclaimed, "Perfect shot; you got him," as all four rams bolted down the brook. I was sure the shot had been true and Jordon's words were reassuring, but I needed to see the effects of my bullet. I quickly moved uphill and forward so I could look down the slope. Seconds later, the ram dropped and began sliding in the snow, coming to rest at the top of a ten-foot waterfall. I had another bighorn sheep with my muzzleloader! My watch read 11:40am. Jordon and I embraced and congratulated each other on our collective success. We couldn't have been more pleased. The emotions felt in such situations are often unexpected, a product of the unique set of circumstances attendant to each hunt. On this occasion, for whatever reason, I experienced the pure joy of a kid on Christmas morning.

Before Jordon and I could put our hands on the ram, we needed to retrace our steps and retrieve the gear we had temporarily abandoned. That accomplished, the two of us made our way to where the ram had come to rest. All the while, I kept yammering on about how I couldn't wait to hold the ram's horns. The ram was magnificent—the horns featured a configuration typical of bighorns, good mass and length, and his pelt was a rich chocolate-brown color.

The setting was idyllic from a photographic standpoint. With the snow-covered mountain and sparse timber as a backdrop, the creek and its series of waterfalls gave the scene visual interest. We made sure to take full advantage of the natural beauty afforded us. As Jordon had intimated, the shot placement had been perfect, centering the lungs. Our next task was to salvage enough cape for a shoulder mount and secure the edible meat. Those jobs accomplished, we loaded our packs for the trip down the mountain.

Jordon and I had worked hard to get our ram, but we had been fortunate, also. I'm the type of person who always thinks about the "what ifs." I don't dwell on them because I realize luck works both ways. Even so, as I left the site of our success, it wasn't lost on me that had we taken a few minutes longer to reach the rock from which I shot, the errant breeze would have prematurely given our position away and the stalk would have failed. Perhaps it's this constant dance of time and circumstance that makes hunting so special.

The trek back to our campsite only took an hour. After resting there briefly, we gathered the remainder of our gear and started the hike back to the truck. All told, Jordon and I covered the six miles separating the kill site from the truck in about three hours. Compared to our ordeal in the dark three years earlier, this effort seemed almost pleasant. I didn't feel even a twinge of guilt for having an easier time of it. That's not to say that soreness, fatigue and blistered feet weren't part of the experience.

Jordon and I pulled up to the lodge exactly six hours after the ram had fallen, setting off another round of celebrations with our wives. I could see Natasha and Janet through the window. Natasha came out first, inquisitively seeking some sign which would indicate the reason for our return, and hoping the news wasn't bad. When Jordon flashed Natasha the "thumbs-up" signal and began backing the truck up to the meat shed, the shrieking and hollering began in earnest! Shortly thereafter, the four of us were exchanging hugs and reliving the day's exciting events. Having Janet immediately at hand to share my good fortune was icing on the cake of an eventful day.

Janet and I still had several days available to us before we were scheduled to fly home. I was glad I hadn't been forced to push the hunt to the limit, especially when the weather turned significantly colder. The temperature dropped to below freezing in camp, and it had to be colder still in the mountains. I was grateful not to be stuck in a tent or shivering on some windblown frozen slope.

Among other things, Jordon and I used the time at our disposal to submit the horns for the compulsory inspection and to attend to other chores. On October 11th, the Aaslands celebrated Canada's Thanksgiving Day at the lodge. Janet and I were honored to be among the family and friends invited to this special occasion. After one more relaxing day, it was time to return home.

The ticket agent at the airport was determined not to allow my sheep to get on the plane. There seemed to be an endless stream of rules and regulations, and each time one requirement was met, another reason to deny transport was produced. Fortunately, Jordon's father was a local taxidermist and Natasha was still with Janet and me. I knew Natasha would guard the ram with her life, and Jordon's dad would do what was required to preserve the cape. I'd just have to wait for my trophy to be shipped to me later.

With the exception of a single ticket agent, the trip to British Columbia had been a resounding success. When I had reassured Jordon two years earlier that we could only add to our previous experience together, little did I know how big the contribution would be. Jordon and I may not have bettered our first hunt together, but we certainly equaled it in terms of the quality of the ram we took and the overall experience. Having Janet along to share in the excitement was an added bonus.

A mature bighorn ram is arguably the most-prized big-game animal in North America. Compared to the other sheep species, the bighorn is often described as the "hard one" to take. On two hunts with Jordon Aasland, I had killed two great rams with an iron-sighted muzzleloader. Furthermore, when the length of both of the shots I had taken was added together, the total shooting distance barely exceeded 100 yards. That's pretty special! For that, Jordon deserves much of the credit. But even he would readily acknowledge that we had been fortunate, as would I. Sometimes in life, unseen forces act to influence the outcome of events. For these two storybook hunts, I was left with the sense that Jordon and I had ridden a wave not entirely of our making.

This was the view we had as we watched the four rams the day before I got my chance.

Bighorn country in British Columbia.

A magnificent bighorn ram in a magnificent setting.

Photo by Jordon Aasland

DESERT BIGHORN SHEEP—2009

Prior to my bighorn hunt in British Columbia, I had contacted Ty Miller of El Fuerte Outfitters regarding the possibility of hunting desert bighorns in the Baja California region of Mexico. I had originally learned about Ty's operation while watching bow hunter Fred Eichler's television program. The sheep habitat looked awesome and Ty catered to bow hunters, so I knew taking a ram with a muzzleloader was certainly within the realm of the possible.

I had expected to wait another year for the hunt to take place, but when Ty called with an opening for March of 2009, I couldn't turn down his offer. As the hunt neared, though, I began to feel some anxiety about the arrangements. Documents which I was supposed to have in hand didn't arrive as promised. Ty assured me everything would be fine once I reached Mexico, so I trusted him and got on the plane.

When I stepped off the jet in Cabo San Lucas, at the southernmost tip of the Baja Peninsula, Ty was waiting for me in the Mexican Customs section of the airport. I breathed a big sigh of relief as Ty and I shook hands for the first time. The visit with the Customs officials was uneventful, and we were soon on our way north towards the hunting area. In the vehicle, Ty handed me the gun powder he had purchased for my muzzleloader, relieving me of my final source of worry. As we rode, Ty filled me in on the difficulties he had been having with the indigenous people who controlled the hunting permits.

I would be hunting an area referred to as Ejido #3, which was located on the eastern side of the Peninsula north of La Paz, bordering the Sea of Cortez. An ejido is an area of land managed in a communal or cooperative manner by its inhabitants. This was Ty's initial business relationship with this particular group of people, although he had longstanding ties to some of the other ejidos. Obviously, there were still some rough spots between the parties which hadn't yet been ironed out.

After a couple hours of driving, much of it on a washboard gravel road, we arrived at camp just before dark. I met the hunting crew which, in conformance with Mexican tradition, was quite large. Jose was the chief guide, while Victor, Juan Antonio and Kiki served as assistants. Ty's father-in-law Buck was in charge of the camp and Guillermo did the cooking for everyone. After introductions and supper, Ty returned to Cabo. When I left home the temperature was about 10° Fahrenheit; at camp the mercury was in the mid-eighties.

The camp wasn't as plush as the ranch houses in Sonora, but it was more than adequate. I even had my own stand-alone tent to sleep in. After breakfast the next morning, Rolando and Geronimo from the ejido showed up to finalize the hunt details. Rolando was the agent for the ejido. Geronimo was familiar with the area, so he would be hunting with us, helping Ty's guides navigate through the unfamiliar terrain. With everyone sure of their role, it was time to go hunting.

The entourage piled into two vehicles for the trip down the highway. After a few miles, we exited the road and entered a long canyon. In the course of the day we found a few sheep, but nothing worth hunting. At one point, I was writing in my diary when Jose called me over. I stumbled while walking with my reading glasses on, and caught my fall by impaling my left hand on a saguaro cactus. That wasn't very bright! I was left with several thorns imbedded in my palm. We returned to camp for the night after a solid first day of hunting.

The Baja was certainly desert habitat and this location contained most of the same plant species I had seen in Sonora, but the vegetation wasn't as dense. Another difference was the presence of numerous canyons, especially at the bases of the mountains. The canyons were quite deep, and they often forked or doubled back on themselves. These features sometimes made it difficult to maintain a directional bearing. It often seemed as though we were walking in a maze. The canyon walls exposed layers of soil, as well as some very interesting geologic oddities. For instance, there were places where smooth bedrock, often in shades of green or pink, would be interrupted by a small cave-like section. These areas were honeycombed in appearance, indicating that the material that had been washed away eons ago was disproportionately susceptible to the effects of water when compared to the surrounding bedrock.

On the second day of hunting our party, consisting of Jose, Juan Antonio, Kiki, Geronimo and me, was driven to another canyon further down the highway. This time, however, we had to hike on foot up the draw. We spent the day exploring as much of the interior as we could, but despite our best efforts we only saw a single ewe and her lamb. We covered quite a bit of ground in the heat, with full packs. It was necessary to carry all the drinking water we would need, as natural sources were few, far between and of questionable quality. At the end of the day, we walked out to the highway for a pre-arranged ride back to camp.

As we waited, Geronimo had a discussion with the people who lived next to the drainage we used to access the road. They had seen two good rams a couple of days earlier, so when our ride showed up, instead of going back to camp, we were transported further to the south. That change in plans would allow us look over more country, and hopefully find the rams. We subsequently hiked into the mountains and camped for the night next to a small natural watering hole. No tents were needed, as it was plenty warm enough and there was no expectation of rain.

Our glassing efforts late that afternoon and the next morning yielded no sightings of the rams or any other sheep. Rather than wasting more time tramping through seemingly sheep-less terrain, after half a day of hunting, we walked back out to the road for another scheduled pick-up. We spent the middle of the day in camp before departing for new hunting grounds around 4pm. This time, our access point off the highway was further north than we had been previously. We hiked for a couple of hours before plopping down in a good camping spot for the night.

Compared to Sonora, the hunting in this part of Mexico was considerably more strenuous. For the most part, we were on foot all day. Everyone needed their backpack, gear and water, and we did a lot of climbing in very hot conditions. The cost of my hunt included a guest. From what I had heard, I didn't think the amenities were such that Janet would enjoy the experience, but the hunt sounded easy enough that I entertained the idea of bringing someone who had never hunted sheep before. After a few days of tougher-than-expected hunting, I was glad I had come alone. It would have been unfair—and possibly disastrous—to throw someone who was unaccustomed to such rigors into the mix.

The mosquitoes were annoying where we had camped, preventing a good night's sleep, at least for me. When we rose the next morning, the sky was overcast and a strong breeze was present. These developments were welcome relief from the non-stop heat we had been experiencing. Despite the change in weather, however, we saw no corresponding improvement in sheep sightings for almost the entire day. But just before sunset, a nice ram appeared on the very top of an adjoining mountain! We didn't have enough daylight remaining to immediately follow up on our find, but we finally had a hot prospect for the coming day.

The ram was in roughly the same location early the next morning. When he fed over the top of the mountain and out of sight, the entire crew wasted no time in improving our position. Using one of the canyons, we worked our way to the backside of the peak where the ram had been seen last. Once there, it wasn't long before one of the Mexicans found the ram above us in the rocks. I loaded the muzzleloader and grabbed my rangefinder, a speedloader in case I needed a follow-up shot, and my "cheat" sheet. This final piece of vital equipment would help me determine the proper sight picture for various shooting distances and angles from the horizontal. Everything else would stay with Geronimo and Kiki in the dry streambed.

Jose was in the lead as we ascended, followed by Juan Antonio and me. I wasn't aware of the ram's exact location relative to the topography, nor did I know what to expect. The language barrier didn't allow for much discussion, either. I was forced to rely on body language and common sense to inform me as to how the stalk was proceeding. As we climbed, I immediately noticed two things: we had the wind in our face and this side of the mountain was as thick with plant life as any place I had seen thus far.

I sensed that we were closing in on the ram, but I still didn't know his precise whereabouts. Suddenly, I felt the wind swap direction. At the same time, Jose was motioning me forward to the large rock that he stood behind. At first, I didn't feel any particular sense of urgency, but when I peeked over the boulder I immediately saw two sheep staring at us. One of them was the ram we sought and the other was a ewe, which I didn't even know existed. The sheep were clearly alerted to our presence, and they could hardly be distinguished from the sea of heavy brush which surrounded them.

I quickly pointed the rangefinder at the ram, which was higher on the slope. The reading came back at 147 yards, with almost no difference in elevation. For that shot, I didn't need to refer to my "cheat" sheet; I knew the proper hold. I immediately dropped to a semi-prone position on the rock, and found a shooting lane to the ram. That task was easier said than done, as I had to make sure the muzzle cleared the rock as well as an array of smaller twigs immediately in front of the gun.

I was ready to shoot, but the ram was facing me directly head-on, and that wasn't a presentation I was comfortable with at that distance. A couple of seconds later, the ram turned to his left as he prepared to vacate the area. I knew that my chance to kill him would be over by the time he took a second step. In the split second the ram was positioned broadside, I adjusted my aim and carefully finished my trigger pull. The ram disappeared into the brush before I recovered from the recoil.

From the moment I first laid eyes on the ram until I sent the bullet on its way, I don't believe more than thirty seconds elapsed. The sight picture had looked good at the instant the gun discharged, but the ram was in motion and I was hurried. I couldn't be positive the bullet had found its mark. Juan Antonio encouraged me to reload, but before I could even get my ramrod free, there was hollering from the creek bed well below us. Kiki had seen the ram go down as he watched events unfold through the spotting scope!

I don't enjoy waiting for hours before being able to shoot at an animal because the pressure tends to build with each passing minute. However, I can't say I preferred working on this tight a schedule either. It would have been nice to have a little more time at my disposal than what I was given in this particular situation. Nevertheless, I was thrilled to have taken my ram, and relieved that I had executed so well in difficult circumstances. I was also grateful for the opportunity. Jose, Juan Antonio and I celebrated before making our way over to the ram. Kiki and Geronimo began climbing to meet us at the ram's resting place.

The ram hadn't traveled forty yards, and we found him wedged up against some brush along the sheep trail he was using to flee the area. The ram sported a beautiful dark gray coat. His horns exhibited a reddish hue, most likely as a result of rubbing the native trees and plants, and the headgear was quite massive and severely broomed. The tips of the horns were as thick as my wrists. Despite my uncertainty, the bullet had been perfectly centered on the lungs.

Once everyone was assembled, it took quite a while to take pictures, as everyone had their own camera. Plus, the place was so steep that just standing in place was a challenge. I wanted to carry the horns, but my Mexican friends would have none of that. I managed to sneak a small bag of meat and a few items of gear that belonged to the guides into my pack. With many able bodies on hand, no one carried too heavy a burden. Once we were loaded up, we made our way down to the streambed before retracing our steps back to the previous night's camping spot to gather the remainder of our belongings. From there, we had a long walk back to the road, where Buck was expected to meet us around 5pm.

The ram had been killed around 10am. I can't remember killing a sheep earlier in the day. It took a couple of hours to get down off the mountain, and another three and a half hours to walk to our rendezvous spot. As we topped the last rise before reaching the road, the cell phones came out. By the time Buck arrived he, Ty and probably everybody else on the Peninsula, was aware of our success. On the way back to camp, we stopped at a small roadside store for some cold soft drinks. We pulled into camp just before dark. From a logistical standpoint, things couldn't have worked out better. I cleaned up the gun before we sat down to a fabulous meal of sheep back straps.

The first order of business on March 10th was a well-deserved shower. People were coming and going all day, as the transition from my hunt to the next one brought changes in personnel. Among the notable arrivals were Ty and Rolando, who were both pleased that we had taken such a good ram. Rolando took the horns to the government office to obtain the required inspection and expedite the permits. Ty had already informed Janet of our good fortune. He left later in the day with Buck, who was headed home. That night, I shared my sleeping quarters with Larry Lewis, who was next in line to kill a desert sheep.

After breakfast the next morning Victor, Juan Antonio, Kiki and I drove to La Paz to meet Ty. We ate lunch at a small shop, where I expressed my appreciation to the guys for a job well done. Ty served as interpreter. Unfortunately, Jose was out hunting with Larry and couldn't attend. After final farewells, Ty and I drove back to Cabo, where I met his wife and two young girls.

My trip home, which began the next morning, was a complete disaster. My second flight left Houston late, causing me to miss my flight from Little Rock and stranding me overnight at the airport. Things didn't go much smoother the next day, but I did get home by 7pm. Unfortunately, I ate some bad pasta in Newark's Liberty airport while waiting for my final flight. By 10pm, I was sick—really sick! I was just grateful that the onset was delayed until I was home, as I couldn't imagine being on a plane and feeling that poorly. My illness lasted for days and it caused me more weight loss than the hunt had.

When I left for Mexico I was hoping that my trust in Ty Miller was well deserved. I wasn't disappointed. He had come through for me at every juncture, and I had a great experience in Baja California. At the start of the hunt, I figured this would be my last trip to Mexico, for any reason. As I left Mexico, though, my perspective had changed. I hoped I could return and hunt with Ty and these same guides, all of whom I now considered friends.

In less than three years, I had taken Dall, Rocky Mountain bighorn and desert bighorn rams. Each of the hunts was very different, but all three shared at least one common element: they ended with a single shot. With my new equipment, I was performing like a well-oiled machine. I was now poised to complete my second Grand Slam® with a muzzleloader. My first slam had ended with the taking of a Rocky Mountain bighorn; a desert bighorn had completed my second slam. A single Stone ram was all that stood between me and my latest goal.

One of the many dry canyons we used to get around the country. These places also provided shade from the sun.

In many places, the rock exibited an interesting honeycombed appearance.

A heavily broomed desert bighorn sheep from Baja California.
Photo by Jose Dolores Aguiar Veliz

Fannin Sheep—2009

After my Rocky Mountain bighorn hunt in British Columbia, I started looking for a Stone sheep hunt for the following year. The desert sheep hunt in Baja California became an "extra" affair, where timing and the availability of permits dictated the scheduling. I had never hunted in the Yukon Territory of Canada before, so I started my search there. Some of the outfitters had Stone sheep roaming their hunting concessions. Generally, the Stone sheep in the Yukon were much lighter in color than their counterparts in British Columbia. Stone sheep which were predominately white in color but had black tails and some gray about the saddle area were also referred to as Fannin sheep. The prevailing wisdom dismissed the idea that a Fannin was a distinct species of sheep, however.

I finally settled on Midnight Sun Outfitting, run by Alan and Mary Ellen Young, for my hunt. Alan was a board member of FNAWS at the time, and the Young's huge hunting area purportedly held plenty of good Fannin rams. My hunt was scheduled for the first of August. Being that far north that close to the summer solstice meant that the hours of daylight would be near their maximum, thus making the outfit's name quite apropos.

I started my journey north on July 27th, arriving in Whitehorse at 2am the next day. My next flight to Dawson City was scheduled for 7am, so I figured I'd just wait in the airport. However, the facility closed shortly after my flight landed. I just took my bags outside, put on a sweater and laid down on a nearby bench until the place reopened. I caught my flight to Dawson City, where Mary Ellen was waiting for me. After a short drive to the center of town, I checked into one of the local hotels. I spent the rest of the day relaxing and recovering from the thirty hours of travel.

The next day featured much of the same, but with the welcome addition of Cass Gebbers and his son Clay, who arrived in the morning and were also hunting with the Youngs. The Gebbers were from Washington State, where Cass ran the family's six-generation apple and cherry farm. Cass had actually been here previously on a hunt with his older son. I spent some time exploring the town, which sits on the banks of the Yukon River. Dawson City was a thriving entity during the gold rush. Both days in town featured exceptionally hot weather, with temperatures close to 90 degrees.

Our charter flight into Hart Lake, the outfit's base of operations, was scheduled for the morning of July 30th. The four of us were at the airport by 9am. Although the plane was a little late in picking us up, the hour-long flight had us in camp before noon. There to greet us was the rest of the Young family: teenagers Jessie and Logan, as well as Alan. The facilities were quite extensive. There were cabins for gear, meat and trophies, sleeping and showering. The centerpiece, though, was a new log lodge overlooking the lake. Alan used horses for some hunts, and he also flew the area, using separate planes for liquid and solid landings.

The first thing I noticed was how big the country was. Hart Lake sat in the middle of a very wide valley, with towering pale mountains at the sides. Most of the mountains didn't appear too rugged, but that wasn't universally true. Jagged peaks could be found without effort. There was one feature which applied to all the mountains: it was a long way from the valley floors to the tops—as much as 3,000 feet. While spruce trees could be found at lower elevations, the area around the lake was dominated by willows and alders. These shrubs quickly petered out as elevation was gained, giving way to the low-growing grasses and weeds that populated the lower slopes of the hills. A little higher, and even these last vestiges of plant life couldn't survive, leaving only bare ground and rocks on the upper reaches of the impressive mountains.

After supper, Alan was going to fly me out to the area I would be hunting. My guide was already there. In the interim, I took the opportunity to organize my gear so I'd be ready to go. There was plenty of time to relax, though. Cass and I had discovered that we were political and philosophical kindred spirits before we left Dawson. At the dinner table, we entertained everyone with political rants. Part of the routine involved his initial reaction to learning that I lived in Massachusetts. Over the years, when I was introduced to other hunters in far-away hunting camps, my place of residence invariably provoked skeptical stares from those who hailed from vastly more conservative locales. Once my new acquaintances understood that I couldn't stand Ted Kennedy any more than they, all was well.

Around 8pm, Alan and I hopped in his Super Cub and headed to the Hart Mine. The flight was a visual feast, and the turbulence was minimal. Ryan Phillips met us at the landing strip. After Alan left, Ryan and I walked a well-worn path the half mile to what would be our base of operations. The Hart Mine had been the site of a serious mining venture decades ago, only to be abandoned more recently. The place was littered with empty 55-gallon drums, rusting equipment and other now-useless tools of the trade. There were several buildings on site, mostly metal pre-fabricated boxes. The place may have been cluttered, but we had a roof over our heads, comfortable sleeping quarters and a small wood stove to provide heat. The entrance to the mine could be seen half way up the mountain to our front.

Ever since my arrival in the Yukon, the temperatures had been unusually warm. Forest fires had been burning throughout the Territory and to the west in Alaska. When we awoke the next morning, a smoky haze filled the valley, reducing visibility. Ryan decided to take a tent up the valley several miles, so we could camp closer to where he expected to find sheep. After establishing camp and dumping some gear, we went looking for rams. The day turned hot once again, and the only animal we discovered was a solitary cow caribou at the very top of the mountain we climbed. We were able to sneak to within fifteen yards of her before she decided to walk off.

Ryan and I had put in a workmanlike day. We probably walked twelve miles, including 2,500 feet of climbing. On foot, the mountains were as big as they had looked from the air. There was a lot more relief from the valley floors to the tops than most of the places I had hunted, but for the most part, the footing wasn't tough or dangerous. The next day was August 1st, the official opening of the hunting season, and I was eager for its arrival.

Unfortunately, the two of us didn't get to hunt the next day, or the day after, or the day after that! A combination of rain, smoke and low clouds conspired to sock in the tops of the mountains, making glassing impossible. We spent the first day in the tent. Halfway into the second day, we made a tactical retreat to the relative comfort of the buildings. On the third day, the rain let up just enough to allow a visit to the mine, where the clouds still concealed everything higher than the entrance. Amazingly, there were sheep tracks entering and exiting the black hole in the hill. Late in the day, conditions started to improve, so we hiked back up to our tent in the hope that we'd be able to resume hunting in the morning.

Ryan and I got up around 6am on the morning of August 4th, and the visibility was pretty darn good. Finally, things were looking up. We climbed to the top of the mountain to our east. Although it wasn't particularly rough going, the trip took a couple of hours. Once we gained the top, we swung north and began making our way down the ridgeline, glassing on both sides of the spine as we went. Almost immediately, Ryan spotted two rams far to our north, well above the mine. The sheep were still a long ways off, requiring us to get much closer before we could evaluate their trophy potential.

Ryan and I needed another two hours to close the distance, as we navigated the ups and downs of several intermediate peaks along the crest of the ridge. The rams were out of sight this entire time, and in some places, the going was a little bit tricky. Nevertheless, we eventually gained a position that allowed us a good look at the rams' last known location, but they had moved elsewhere. It was time for lunch, so we took a break. If the rams didn't pop into view shortly, we'd just have to go looking for them.

When the rams didn't show in a timely manner, Ryan and I decided to get more aggressive. We figured they probably hadn't moved too far, so we planned to carefully shift our location so we could see into the nearby places which remained hidden from view. We spent most of the afternoon scouring every conceivable nook and cranny that may have held the rams, but to no avail. Apparently, the duo had decided to leave the immediate country. It was late in the day, and we had given up a lot of elevation in the effort to find the rams. We decided to call it a day.

About a third of the way down the mountain, as I was navigating a rocky gully, I placed my right foot on a large stone which shifted unexpectedly. I lost my balance. As I fell, my left leg was positioned beneath me with my foot bent at an awkward angle. My entire body weight, as well as that of my pack, was directed to my oddly aligned foot. I thought I heard something snap as I crashed to the ground, but there was no mistaking the pain I felt! After I regained my breath I tested the injury. I could put weight on the leg, but the ankle wasn't very stable and pain was significant.

Ryan and I were still a long way from the bottom, and I knew it was going to be a challenge just getting down. I quickly discovered that it was impossible to descend facing forward, so I had to back down the mountain one step at a time, relying primarily on my right leg. I used my gun to provide additional support and painstakingly lowered myself until we were on level ground. It was exhausting work, both physically and mentally. Around 7pm, I limped into the former mining camp, concluding a grueling thirteen hours of hunting in which we had both climbed and descended approximately 4,000 vertical feet.

In the comfort of camp, I removed my boot and took my first look at the ankle. It was already bruised in several places and visibly swollen. I applied ice and took a couple of ibuprofen tablets, but I knew the ankle would be worse come morning no matter what I did for it. At the very least, I had severe sprains in multiple locations. Given my condition, I didn't have any idea how I could do what was required of me, and resigned myself to the fact that my hunt was, for all intents and purposes, over.

The ankle's appearance wasn't as bad as I had expected the next day, but that hardly mattered. I could limp along over flat ground, but any unevenness in the terrain presented problems, even without weight on my back. We were forced to spend the entire day in camp, wasting a day that featured perfect weather. That night, I used the satellite phone to call Hart Lake, leaving a message informing the Youngs of my predicament.

On August 6th, with the ankle no worse than the day before, I decided to give it a try. Ryan and I went back up the hill where the rams had been two days earlier. As long as I had a flat spot to place my foot, I could climb. Anything that resulted in lateral twisting or instability was painful. Worse yet, my ankle was so weak that I was constantly in danger of losing my balance and falling. Through will power and concentration I was able to climb 1,500 feet, but I was very slow. We didn't find any sheep, so we returned to camp around 1pm. I was exhausted from the effort. Later in the afternoon, Ryan and I observed two ewes descend to the mine entrance and disappear inside. An hour later they emerged from the dark hole. Whether they had been attracted by the water, the coolness or lingering minerals, there's no way to tell.

Despite my limitations, Ryan and I decided to try and access the country west of camp come morning. When we awoke, however, the whole valley was socked in once again, thwarting our plans. About supper time, the distinctive sound of an approaching plane could be heard. Alan had come to check on us. After a brief discussion, we agreed that the lodge would be the best place for me, so I packed up my gear and jumped into the plane. After depositing me at Hart Lake, Alan returned for Ryan.

Ryan and I had hoped to use the horses to hunt some of the sheep country close to the lodge, but the steeds had vanished during the night. With Alan's assistance in the air, the animals were found, but it took Ryan five hours to get them back to the lodge. The day's hunt was ruined, but getting a sheep would have been a long shot anyway. About 8pm, the rest of the crew returned from their hunt. Clay had taken a pretty ram on the very first day but Cass had shot a monster: 44 inches long and big enough to make the Boone & Crockett record book. The entire group was jubilant. After hearing the story, I described their experience as "the greatest father-

and-son hunt of all time." I was extremely happy for both of them, but their good fortune also served to magnify my miserable plight.

Cass, Clay and I flew back to Dawson City on August 10th, where we spent the night before catching our flight to Whitehorse the next morning. My next flight was later in the day, so I stayed at the airport. Cass and Clay weren't leaving until the following day, so we said our goodbyes. The rest of my trip was uneventful, and I arrived home around mid-day on August 12th.

In my journal, the last entry read, "The worst trip of my life, with no one really at fault." I couldn't have been more disappointed. I had prepared diligently for this hunt and I had much riding on it. Yet, bad weather and one unfortunate step limited me to a single day of effective hunting. My investments of time, sweat and money had yielded mostly painful memories of how cruel the mountains can be. I never had my ankle checked, as it gradually and continuously improved. Seven months would pass before it felt normal again, though.

The very big mountains of the Yukon Territory. Large bowls and vertical relief in excess of 2,000 feet were the norm.

Guide Ryan Phillips can be seen climbing among some large rock outcroppings at the very top of the mountain, hours before I fell and injured my ankle.

This is the entrance to the abandoned Hart Mine. We saw sheep disappear into the hole and re-emerge an hour later.

Cass Gebbers (l) and his son Clay (r) with two fantastic rams from the Yukon.

Stone Sheep—2010

When I returned home from the Yukon, I was obsessed with redeeming the sad state of affairs I found myself in. I immediately began searching for a place to hunt in 2010. The Youngs were nice people and they had done their best for me, but they hadn't spoken to me about returning and given my experience, I didn't exactly have a warm fuzzy feeling about the place. Besides, getting to the Yukon was a logistical nightmare for me. Extra travel days had to be built into the itinerary, and no matter how carefully I planned my commercial flights, the airlines could screw everything up at the last minute by changing their schedule. I decided to concentrate my efforts on British Columbia instead.

    I eventually settled on Guy Anttila's Big Game Hunts out of Atlin, British Columbia. Guy only took a couple of sheep hunters each year, and unlike many other outfitters, no horses were needed to access his area. From my discussions with Guy and some of his recent clients, getting within muzzleloader range didn't seem to pose a problem. At Guy's suggestion, I scheduled my trip for the first hunt of the year, as the weather could be expected to be more stable. Less than a month after leaving the Yukon, my plans were set for the following year. I still faced eleven long months of waiting before I'd get the chance to quell the bitter taste in my mouth.

The months passed slowly, but I finally left home on July 30th. Whitehorse was once again my destination. I was supposed to overnight there, and then be picked up the next morning for the two-hour drive south to Atlin. Unfortunately, due to flight delays, I spent the night in Calgary and didn't get into Whitehorse until mid-day. Even so, my transportation was there when I arrived, and we quickly departed for the Anttila residence. Guy and his wife Elsie greeted me warmly. After a home-cooked meal, I organized my gear and donned hunting attire for the short flight into Sandy Lake in Guy's float-equipped Super Cub.

There to meet me was my guide, Devin Jewell, along with Scott Mackenzie. Scott was in the process of acquiring the business from Guy and Elsie, and he would be spending time in the field with us. That was fine with me, as Scott was an experienced guide, outfitter and hunter, and his presence could only serve to improve my prospects. The three of us had a serious climb ahead of us, mostly through brush wet from recent rain. We had a decent trail to hike on, but the exertion made for sauna-like conditions inside the rain gear we wore. Around 8pm, we finally broke out of the brush and into the alpine. We climbed a little higher to the campsite and waiting tents. Upon our arrival, it started raining in earnest, so we called it an early night and dove into our shelters, which also gave us protection from the plentiful insects.

The three of us had climbed approximately 1,500 feet to reach the tents, which were pitched in a high saddle at the head of adjoining drainages. From this place, another 1,000 feet of elevation remained before the long parallel ridgelines on each side could be reached. Devin and Scott had been looking for rams up here for a couple of days, and they had seen some good prospects in the vicinity of the camp. On our first day, we looked over the country on both sides of camp, but we couldn't find the rams. We did see a bunch of mountain goats and several mountain caribou. There was no shortage of mosquitoes, though. With no breeze to keep them at bay and warmer-than-normal temperatures, I was bitten hundreds of times.

As I stood at the top of the mountain, I could better appreciate the lay of the land. The dominant geographical feature was Atlin Lake to our east, which was a huge body of water that could be seen from most high vantage points. We occupied Atlin Mountain, which contained several ridges and numerous basins. The immediate area held plenty of sheep habitat, but it was clear that the mountainous terrain was fairly isolated. As I looked to the north, west and south, the landscape quickly changed to hills and lowlands more suitable to bears and moose. Much of the high country was covered in rock, including some impressive boulder fields. This made for challenging walking at times.

Two resident hunters (the first such intrusion in ten years) were known to be hunting the area, and although we hadn't seen them in our travels, it was possible that they had somehow spooked the rams that Scott and Devin had located prior to my arrival. We decided to take another good look around in the morning. If nothing turned up, we'd go back to the lake and get Guy to move us elsewhere. We did see one sub-legal ram close to camp but nothing else. After another half a day of hunting, we followed through with our plan, leaving the immediate area to the resident hunters.

Guy transported the three of us to Rupert Lake, where we then took a four-wheeler about seven miles in a circuitous route to the backside of the mountain behind Sandy Lake. As we approached our ultimate destination, two blond grizzly bears could be seen digging some distance away in an adjoining valley. We hardly had camp erected when we started seeing rams on the upper reaches of the nearby mountains. There were at least two different groups of sheep, with at least one legal ram in each band. These findings portended improved prospects for the coming day.

August 3rd featured a buffet of animals. First, as I went to fill my water bottle early in the morning, I encountered one of the grizzly bears digging for gophers less than 200 yards from our tents. Next, as we climbed, a group of ten lambs and ewes passed within sixty yards of us, headed in the opposite direction. Once we gained the ridge and looked into a basin on the off side, we discovered a band of five rams lying in the snow below. None of the rams were legal, however. Finally, we found a single ram nestled on another patch of snow further down the ridge. The sheep were obviously taking advantage of the snow to provide relief from the warm temperatures and to escape the swarms of insects.

I really thought we were going to kill this last ram. The three of us were above the ram and used the cover of a rock field to sneak to within 150 yards of him. Unfortunately, once we got into shooting position, Devin didn't think the ram was quite legal. It was too bad, as the stalk had put us well within range and the ram didn't have a clue that he was in danger. If the ram had been a year older, the hunt might have ended right there.

With regards to animal sightings, the next day ended up being almost a complete bust. Where all the sheep from the previous day had gone remained a mystery. The bugs were less prevalent, as a strong breeze kept them from landing. We were able to view the resident hunters waiting for a plane to pick them up at Sandy Lake, so they must have killed at least one ram. Unable to find sheep, we decided to relocate camp again. Using the four-wheeler, we headed south a few miles across an open plain to Gopher camp, arriving around 5pm.

The move to Gopher afforded us the comfort of a wood cabin, but more importantly, access to a separate and distinct parcel of sheep habitat. The next day, we took the all-terrain vehicle to the base of the mountain and began our climb. Once on top, it was apparent that this country was quite different from where we had been hunting. The foothills we occupied had pockets of snow in numerous places, but these hills backed up to a more formidable spine of mountains enveloped in snow and ice. To me, this juxtaposition of mountains and scenery constituted classic sheep range more reminiscent of Alaska than British Columbia.

The day was beautiful. The sun was out, it wasn't too hot and a steady breeze kept the mosquitoes away. I took a lot of pictures of the gorgeous surroundings. The three of us were able to cruise ridgelines all day, glassing into the adjoining basins as we progressed. We did see fourteen lambs and ewes, a couple of groups of mountain goats and one nice bull caribou. Despite the miles we walked and the untold acres of stellar sheep country we looked at, not one ram was found. Only God knows why this place wasn't crawling with sheep.

Just after dawn on August 6th, it started to rain. Guy flew in to drop off food and to fly Scott out to Atlin, where he was expected to spend a few days with his wife and kids. It poured for most of the day, leaving me grateful that we weren't stuck in a tent somewhere. Devin and I didn't get to hunt, but having the day off wasn't entirely unappreciated, as we had been working extremely hard since my arrival.

The next morning we left Gopher to return to our last camp. We had hoped that our absence and the departure of the resident hunters would cause the sheep to resume their normal routines. Devin and I walked all over the mountain, but we didn't see a single sheep. In fact, I didn't even see any sign that looked like it had been made since our departure three days earlier. We did see a handful of caribou, including three good bulls.

After a discouraging day of hunting, while we still held the high ground, Devin called Guy around 7pm to report on our status. From his house, Guy had been seeing four rams in a basin on the Atlin Lake side of Atlin mountain. Devin and I quickly descended the mountain to camp, packed up and rode the quad three hours back to Rupert Lake, arriving just after dark. Guy would fly in first thing in the morning and move us to Sandy Lake, where we'd be in position to go look for the four rams.

With our return to Sandy Lake, Devin and I had come full circle. After leaving some incidental gear in the cabin, we started the long slog up through the timber and brush. After a brief pause to set up the tent near the top of the timber, we continued our climb up the backside of Atlin Mountain. After 2,500 feet of nearly non-stop exertion, we finally topped out. We thoroughly glassed the interior of one basin but found no sheep. To access the next bowl, we had to traverse a large boulder field.

This was dangerous going. Some of the rocks were as big as refrigerators, and many of them were precariously balanced. There's nothing quite as disconcerting as feeling boulders, which weigh hundreds of pounds each, move as you step on them! To make matters worse, the rocks were covered with lichen. When dry traction was good; once wet, however, it was like walking on wall-paper paste. Half way across the rock slide it began to rain, making for even more treacherous footing. Devin and I eventually exited the boulder field in one piece, but I made it clear that I wasn't going through there again, wet or dry. Either of us could have easily become trapped by an unexpected shift of material, losing a leg—and maybe a life—in the process.

Upon exiting the boulder field, Devin and I were finally able to look down into the basin where Guy had seen the rams. A single ram fed below us, and both of his horns were broken about twelve inches from their origins. The thick stubs replaced what had undoubtedly been more glorious headgear in years past, and made for one of the goofiest looking sheep I had ever seen. The ram's freakish horns had the advantage of eliminating him as a target of our attention, though. After more than a week of hard hunting, the lone mature ram we finally found wasn't even fair game.

Devin and I were up early again the next morning. We hiked straight up the same mountain we climbed the previous day. It was a real struggle to make the top, as the accumulated wear and tear was beginning to take a toll. Once we gained the ridge, we swung to the north in an attempt to see into the country we hadn't covered the day before. After looking over the basins on the Atlin Lake side of the mountain without spotting any animals, Devin decided to glass the ridge on the opposite side of the drainage from where we had initiated our climb.

From our lofty position, Devin was able to find a single ram bedded at the very end of that ridge, at the point where the mountain abruptly transformed to more moderate terrain containing timber below. This ram was mature, but he was missing most of his left horn. Even so, he was the first legal ram I had laid eyes on and we were running out of days to hunt. After taking a good look through the spotting scope, I simply said, "Let's go kill him."

Devin and I quickly descended the steep hillside we had spent so much time and effort to climb, and then struggled up the slope of the opposing ridge. Once on top, we began working our way down the ridgeline towards the ram. We closed to within 600 yards, but couldn't advance further due to lack of cover. After half an hour of waiting behind some rocks, the ram rose from his bed. Within seconds, he walked behind a contour in the mountain and disappeared from our sight.

Seizing our chance, Devin and I dropped our packs and practically ran down the ridge. As we approached the ram's location we slowed to a crawl. Given the terrain and a favorable wind direction, I fully expected to crest the hill and catch the ram feeding below us at very close range. Instead, he was gone! I don't think ten minutes had elapsed from the time we left our hiding place to the moment when we were standing in the ram's bed.

The terrain in this area was exceptionally steep and craggy, and the broken topography limited our ability to see long distances. Figuring the ram couldn't be too far away, Devin and I decided to remain in place in the hope that the ram would pop into view or the sound of falling rock would give away his location. We patiently maintained our vigil for more than an hour without results. Devin then circled below the cliffs in an attempt to discover the ram's whereabouts, also without effect.

It didn't seem possible that the undisturbed ram could have disappeared in so short a period without us either seeing or hearing him. Devin and I were both convinced the ram was hidden nearby. Our only practical option was to continue the waiting game, and I'm sure that's what we would have done had Devin not spotted four rams in the valley floor. They were working their way towards the ridge we occupied.

Of the four, one ram might have been legal, but we needed a better look to know for sure. After a quick conversation, Devin and I decided to retreat to our abandoned packs, where we'd be in a better position to intercept the rams. We'd also have the spotting scope available to help make a final judgment regarding the ram's legal status. For their part, the rams seemed content to mill about low on the hill. We used the ridgeline to conceal our movement. About half way back to our packs, two of the smaller rams popped over the ridge and blundered into us. Of course, our presence only served to spook them back down the way they had come. In order to meet us, the rams must have practically galloped up the hill, starting the moment we left for our packs. Unbelievable!

Devin and I waited and watched from the top of the ridge for several more hours, but we never saw any of the five sheep we had encountered earlier. By day's end, I had had enough. I had been running on fumes and adrenaline for a couple of days, and didn't feel like I could climb the mountain come morning. I informed Devin that I was pulling the plug on the hunt, sacrificing our last full hunting day. We descended to our campsite, packed all of our gear and hiked down to the cabin at Sandy Lake, arriving about 10pm. It had been another exhausting day, both physically and mentally.

After spending the night at the cabin, Devin and I were flown back to town the next morning, where we were finally able to hose the accumulated grime off our bodies. We detailed the previous day's events to Guy, who seemed as disgusted as the two of us regarding our bad luck. My legs seemed "rubbery" all day and I developed tremors in my hands whenever I attempted any fine-motor activities. I told Guy I felt the same way I usually do the day after packing a sheep off the mountain. I knew I would recover in short order, but I also knew that my body had been sending me warnings. I was comfortable with my decision not to push myself further and risk a serious mishap.

Devin and I had worked hard enough to earn a nice ram, but it was not to be. For all our efforts, I only saw one ram which was definitely legal. On the heels of the previous year's disaster, this outcome was more than disappointing; it pained me to the core. When I returned from the Yukon one year earlier, I felt an urgency to make amends for the misfortune I had experienced. When I arrived home this time, I was completely ambivalent about hunting sheep. I needed time to digest what had transpired and see just how much "fire" I still had in my sheep-hunting belly.

Scott mentioned the possibility of having me come back for the 2011 season, but he couldn't make a firm commitment until after the current hunting season. We expected to touch base at the Dallas Safari Club convention in January.

That was fine with me. I was perfectly content to wait until then to see if I would be hunting sheep in 2011. If Scott was able to follow through on his offer, then I'd likely return; if not, I figured I would sit 2011 out. I had neither the energy nor the inclination to undertake an immediate search for another Stone sheep outfitter.

An interesting rocky spine with a portion of Atlin Lake below.

Scott Mackenzie and Devin Jewell glassing for sheep from a mountain near Gopher camp.

Guide Devin Jewell looking through the spotting scope at the one-horned ram that ultimately gave us the slip.

Epilogue

Taking that one-horned ram in British Columbia would have made for a perfect ending to this book. I would have achieved my third Grand Slam® and the reader, who hopefully has acquired some emotional investment in the storyline as a result of my writing, could put the book down on a positive note and with a sense of closure. Instead, the reader is understandably left with unanswered questions and a feeling that someone let the air out of the balloon.

Believe me; more than anyone, I wish things had happened differently. But life is rarely that tidy, and we don't always get what we want. Shortly after my sheep hunt in British Columbia, I developed serious problems related to my cervical spine (neck) which left me with significant pain, numbness and deficits of strength in my right arm and shoulder. I subsequently underwent surgery in which two discs were removed and three vertebrae were fused. A metal plate and three large screws provide support to my healing spine. Recovery will take a full year.

As I write, it remains to be seen whether I will ever be capable of hunting sheep again. Post-surgically, loss of upper-body strength is my main problem. There's no question that my sheep-hunter's conditioning helped my recovery from surgery, and for that I'm thankful. While I'm cautiously optimistic that I'll eventually regain most of my former capabilities, progress is slow and there are no guarantees. Besides, I'll be fifty-nine at the next possible hunting opportunity, and who knows what other issues, medical or otherwise, I could be facing by then. Age and infirmity are not assets when climbing mountains! All I can do is maintain a positive attitude and hope that I have at least one good sheep hunt left in me. If I am so blessed, my quest for that elusive Stone ram will resume.

Prologue to the Second Edition

I wrote the original version of this book, which concluded with the epilogue, while I was convalescing from my aforementioned spine surgery. As I stated in the epilogue, at that time, due to the physical deficits I was living with, I wasn't at all certain that sheep hunting would play a role in my future. I could only hope that it would! My recovery proved to be long, trying and incomplete. However, I did regain enough of what I had lost to contemplate a return to the mountains and the renewal of my quest for the heretofore missing Stone ram which would conclude my third Grand Slam®.

The following story details the hunt that marked my re-emergence as a sheep hunter. Despite the additional work involved, I chose to add the new chapter and republish the book. In doing so, I made a conscious decision to keep the original epilogue. While this approach may leave the purists in the book-publishing world scratching their heads, I happen to think being faithful to the actual chronology is more important than any small abuses of style. Plus, tossing the epilogue and simply describing what took place during the hunt would have left the reader with an incomplete record and no foundation for evaluating this adventure in its proper context.

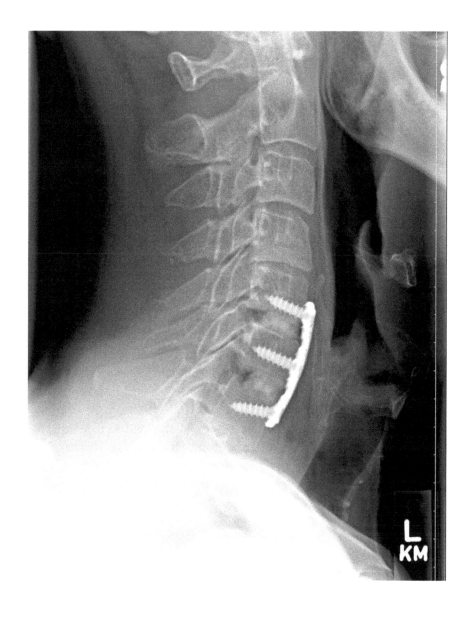

Stone Sheep—2012

In November 2011, about six months after my spine surgery, my surgeon gave me the green light to do some walking with my backpack. I wasn't overly aggressive, limiting myself to hauling a mere thirty pounds. I did well and having the backpack on again also helped improve my overall sense of well-being. For the first time in almost a year I was beginning to feel more like myself. I wasn't yet whole but after several hikes I thought that, given continued progress, I might eventually have what it takes to hunt sheep come 2012, at least physically. Yet, I hadn't fired my muzzleloader in eleven months and I wouldn't be cleared for that activity until the coming April. That would leave me with a few short months to regain my shooting form.

Obviously, I still faced obstacles and unknowns, but I figured I had turned an important corner. I hoped that determined effort could overcome the remaining deficiencies plaguing me in time for the 2012 sheep season. As I contemplated a possible return to sheep country I recalled an old adage: Nothing ventured, nothing gained. And in the final analysis, I don't think I could have lived with myself if I hadn't put aside the uncertainties, pushed myself and made the attempt!

Thus, I began my search for an outfitter who controlled coveted Stone sheep permits. Early on, Jarrett Deuling's name kept surfacing. Jarrett owns Deuling Stone

Outfitters operating out of the Yukon Territory in Canada. Since he took over the hunting concession from Pete Koser in 2009, Jarrett had produced a solid record of success on older-class sheep. By all accounts he was knowledgeable, thorough and energetic in pursuit of the game his clients sought. Equally appealing was the fact that his fee structure had two components: a base fee and a trophy fee, the latter of which was only collected if the hunter was successful. In my eyes, the trophy fee served to incentivize the outfitter to work extra hard; it also acted as a financial hedge should my string of bad luck continue.

    I quickly contacted Jarrett and by the conclusion of our discussion I had a strong sense that the outfit and the area would be a good match for me and my muzzleloader. One problem remained: Jarrett didn't have any openings for 2012. Somewhat reluctantly, I moved on to the other outfits on my list. Much to my surprise, though, within two weeks Jarrett called back, explaining that he had a cancellation and offering me the hunt. After absorbing the details, I quickly made my decision and mailed Jarrett my deposit.

    Come April 2012, I lurched headlong into preparing myself for the fast-approaching hunt. With winter in the rearview mirror, I once again dusted off the backpack and began training in earnest. This part of my preparation seemed very normal and familiar. On the other hand, shooting the gun after such an extended absence felt quite foreign! Because of my surgery it was more difficult to assume my normal shooting posture. Plus, my eyesight didn't seem to be as exacting as it had been when developing the proper sight pictures using the open sights. And as I had feared, time had definitely eroded my abilities behind the gun. I was so rusty that when I attempted to clean the muzzleloader after my first shooting session, I found myself somewhat paralyzed, trying to consciously recall the time-tested sequence which used to come to me automatically!

As the months passed, I made continual progress in recouping my strength and improving my dormant shooting skills. By the time I left for the Yukon on July 28th, I felt confident that I was up to the task. More important, I knew there was nothing else I could have done to prepare myself for what lay ahead. Ultimately, if I failed it wouldn't be because I hadn't worked hard enough! Nevertheless, I departed with very mixed feelings. I was excited about my imminent return to the beauty of the mountains and the prospect of hunting sheep, but I was also filled with a strong sense of anxiousness. Failure was still an option due to any number of reasons, many of them beyond my control. Understandably, nagging self-doubt fueled by my personal encounter with human frailty and impossible-to-ignore bad memories of my last two sheep hunts served to magnify the potential for disappointment.

My flights were relatively uneventful and I arrived in Whitehorse on schedule late in the afternoon on July 28th. There to greet me when I stepped into the airport baggage area was my guide-to-be, Bob House. Bob was was as warm and affable as he was physically imposing. Twenty years my junior, this retired professional hockey player stood a bit over six feet tall and weighed close to 240 pounds. I immediately decided to be nice to Bob, no matter what! As I soon learned, Bob was Jarrett's best friend and personal hunting companion. They had grown up together in Whitehorse. I knew I was in capable hands. All my gear arrived with me in good condition, and Bob possessed the remaining (and arguably the most critical) item I'd need in order to be able to hunt— the TripleSeven powder for my muzzleloader.

Early the next morning Bob and I were flown to Butte Lake, the kick-off point for the hunt. The pilot departed and soon returned with Karla Charlton, who would serve as an assistant guide and packer. It quickly became apparent that Karla was a free-spirited, adventuresome young lady with varied outdoor interests. Ostensibly, she was with us to gain experience hunting sheep. Although it hadn't been said, I figured her main purpose was to bail me out in the event that I couldn't pull my own weight. Whatever her ultimate role proved to be, Karla fit right in and I was glad to have her along.

The lake was only a few miles from the mountains we would hunt. The distance may not have been great, but the ground which stood between us and our destination was among the most brutal and punishing I'd ever experienced! Jarrett had cautioned me about the approximately five-hour trek through an old burn. In my mind, that description conjured an expectation of an uphill fight through brush containing few game trails. It was all that and more! What I wasn't prepared for was the total lack of evenness of footing. Even after we broke out of the jungle, we still had to contend with the ever-present hummocks and other impediments to proper foot placement! Six hours after we started, we finally made camp in a pretty (but still bumpy) setting next to a small alpine lake close to the mountains. I felt like every muscle, tendon and ligament in my body had been twisted and stretched to its breaking point!

As I surveyed the surrounding terrain I didn't see anything that looked too imposing. In fact, the distance from valley floor to mountain top looked to be no more than 1,500 vertical feet, which was significantly less than I had experienced on my last two hunts. On the negative side, the nearby mountains were relatively smooth in texture, lacking an abundance of relief which would allow concealment for muzzleloader-close stalks. For the most part, the mountain slopes consisted of alternating strips of short green vegetation and boulder fields of gray rocks coated with black lichen.

The actual start of the hunting season was still two days away (August 1st). By getting into the hunting area early we could use those days to try and locate legal rams to hunt. On July 30th the three of us went looking for sheep, performing a big traverse of the closest section of the mountain to our north. While we did see a bunch of lambs, ewes and younger rams, no mature rams were located. We also walked past the remains of a very respectable winter-killed mountain caribou, whose intact skull and antlers were marred only slightly by the chewing of rodents.

After a full day on the mountain, spent alternating between climbing and stationary glassing sessions, the three of us returned to the campsite for a meal of freeze-dried fare before turning in for the night. We fully expected to tour another section of the mountain come morning. However, that plan became unnecessary the minute we opened the tent flap early the next day.

Bob, like any good guide, was always on the lookout for sheep. Even though he was barely awake, the first thing Bob did after exiting the tent on July 31st was scan the mountain in front of us. Almost immediately he spotted a band of seven Stone rams which were feeding contentedly along the crest of the nearby peak. Better still, closer inspection employing the spotting scope revealed that one of the rams was a top-end trophy by anyone's standard. With exceptionally even horns, each approximating forty inches and emanating from heavy bases, the obvious dean of the group would easily score in the 160s. Besides his impressive headgear, the ram clearly exhibited the darkest coloration of the bunch, although his head and neck remained pure white. This was just the sort of ram that I had hoped the Yukon held in store for me when I had booked the hunt months earlier.

For most of the morning, we watched the rams from camp until they worked their way around the flank of the mountain. Bob was even able to take several good photos of the group through his spotting scope. After the rams wandered out of sight, we relocated our surveillance post half a mile so we could keep track of the rams for the rest of the day. A small copse of stunted spruce trees effectively screened our presence from the seven sets of watchful eyes. The sheep seemed to be relaxed and content as they alternated between feeding and bedding. I was surprised by two things: the rams were quite active and didn't bed for any length of time, and they stayed fairly low on the mountain.

As the three of us maintained our afternoon vigil, I carefully studied the landscape in the vicinity of the sheep for features of terrain we could use for stalking purposes the next day. I made note of a couple of good ambush points should the rams retrace their steps, as well as a bulge of the mountain which looked like it would provide cover should the sheep move up the valley they currently occupied. Around 8pm the hunting party returned to camp, certain that the rams wouldn't stray far during the few hours of true darkness that existed this far north in late July.

After supper Bob, Karla and I hit the tents, full of anticipation for the coming day. When the alarm sounded at 4:30am, Bob stuck his head out of his sleeping bag and said, "Merry Christmas!" I didn't have to ask him what he meant, but I wasn't allowing myself to celebrate prematurely, either. We still had to re-acquire the rams, get close to them and hope they made a mistake that would allow us to complete a stalk to within range of my muzzleloader. In my mind, all those pieces coming together so neatly was still a pretty tall order, especially since the available topography didn't appear to be particularly conducive to sneaking around sight unseen.

Not un-expectedly, the rams weren't far from where we had left them the night before. We quickly positioned ourselves on the ridge guarding the nearside entrance to the valley in which the sheep had settled, about half way up the mountain. With the rams in their present location we could get no closer than 700 yards. Stymied for the moment, we dropped our packs and continued our surveillance using the plentiful rocks and the curvature of the mountain for cover. After watching and waiting for about an hour, the rams began working their way down to a green patch of vegetation in the valley floor. It was time to make our move!

All three of us quickly gathered our gear and carefully danced our way across the gray, lichen-covered rocks of the extensive boulder field which lay before us. A short side ridge off the main spine, the bulge I had observed the day prior, allowed us to advance without being seen. Before long, we quietly approached the rock-strewn crest which we hoped would put us within range of the big ram. As we peeked over the last obstacle preventing a view of the valley floor, only two of the rams were visible. But, one of them was the only one that mattered! Bob and I simultaneously ranged the big ram at 175 yards, at a moderate downhill shooting angle. That was close enough.

I quickly assumed a sitting shooting position using Bob's pack on top of one of the plentiful rocks to solidify the platform. After waiting a few minutes for the ram to turn broadside, I steadied my aim and touched the trigger when the sight picture looked good. Within seconds, two things became clear: I had hit the ram, but the bullet hadn't been well-placed. Instead of impacting the heart/lungs, which would have caused a quick death, the bullet I had unleashed had struck the ram in the guts! Although the shot was the longest I had ever taken at an animal with my muzzleloader, it was well within my capabilities and I had no explanation—or excuse—as to why I hadn't performed better.

The ram, accompanied by his six buddies, climbed a short way up the opposite slope and quickly bedded. He was obviously hurting, and before long he struggled to keep his head upright. I was fairly certain that we'd eventually claim the ram; I just didn't know how long it would take to do so. As with all gut-shot animals, the best course of action is to be patient and not push the issue. The rams had no idea where we were, so we hunkered in place among the rocks and waited.

About thirty minutes into our watch the ram seemingly breathed his last. That served to release the tension that had been steadily building all morning, as well as fuel an outpouring of emotion tied to events much longer in the making. Tears freely flowed as I reflected upon the disappointments of my past two hunts, my fears that my health might keep me from hunting sheep again, and especially all the hard work I had put in to make this day possible. More than anything, though, I was overwhelmed with a strong sense of gratitude!

Incredibly, about the same time I was regaining my composure, the presumably "dead" ram stirred after being physically prodded by his compatriots! To say that I was stunned might be the understatement of the year. To this point, the ram wasn't situated such that I could have attempted another shot. He was approximately 250 yards from us—the very limit of my range with the muzzleloader—but he was lying in a depression and at least one other ram was always in the line of fire.

Bob, Karla and I were getting cold from lack of movement. That fact, combined with the realization that our wait might be longer than we had first anticipated, resulted in a decision to have Karla descend a few dozen yards and retrieve our abandoned packs and the additional clothing they held. I knew Karla's movement would attract the rams' attention, so I now felt free to reload the muzzleloader. As expected, the rams zeroed in on our location and began to mill about. After a few minutes the wounded ram stood momentarily. The distance between us was now 260 yards, and when he was clear of the other sheep I sent another round his way. Hit for a second time, the ram struggled forward about thirty yards and re-bedded. In short order, the majestic ram was forever freed of his pain. He deserved a better—more humane—end!

It was hard to believe, but it wasn't yet noon on the first day of the hunting season. And Bob had been right all along: With the ram on the ground, for all intents and purposes, it was Christmas morning! As we approached the fallen ram, it was clear that he was every bit as good as hinted at by our first glimpse of him through the spotting scope. Believe me; I'd have been happy with any legal ram. To take one with horns this impressive was an added bonus. The rings on his horns, caused by the cessation of horn growth brought on by winter, bore witness to the fact that the ram had survived eleven winters in this challenging climate. An examination of the ram's teeth confirmed his advancing years. Clearly, it remained an open question whether the ram would made it through another season of scarcity. After admiring our trophy for several minutes, I used Bob's satellite phone to call my wife and share my good news.

If my marksmanship had been found wanting on the first shot, if only by a matter of inches, then my second shot provided some measure of redemption, especially considering the circumstances under which it had been taken. First, I had to take the shot in the immediate aftermath of one of the most severe emotional rollercoasters I've ever experienced. Anticipation during the stalk was followed by escalating apprehension upon wounding the ram. When I became convinced that the ram had expired, I experienced a one-of-a-kind release of tension that had been years in the making. Then, after absorbing the shock that the ram was still alive, I was forced to gather myself and execute. Second, the range exceeded my maximum shooting distance by ten yards. That doesn't sound like a lot when discussing centerfire rifle trajectories, but for heavy, slow-moving projectiles like my 300 grain Dead Center muzzleloading bullet, bullet drop is rapidly accelerating beyond 200 yards. I doubt I would have attempted the same shot on a healthy animal, but I had no such reservations given the fact that the ram was already wounded.

Between us, we had three cameras and they all got plenty of use. After the photo session, as Bob and Karla prepared to skin the ram, I initiated a discussion regarding the type of mount I'd like. I felt a full mount would best preserve the ram for posterity, and we had plenty of daylight to work with. I also knew I could easily lug the horns and full cape back to our lakeside camp. However, once all the rest of my gear and food was added to my pack, I wasn't nearly as confident about the subsequent march from camp to Butte Lake. I didn't want to crap out on the way and impose my load on Bob and Karla. Bob quickly interrupted me by saying, "If you don't have a full mount done, I'll throw you off this mountain!" He was only joking, of course, as he reassured me that, one way or the other, the ram would make it to Butte Lake no matter what my contribution proved to be. Bob's strong and selfless stance sealed the deal: a life-size mount it would be!

The trip off the mountain was the easiest of my sheep-hunting career, lasting about an hour. The three of us spent the next day at camp, as Bob and Karla attended to the cape. While they turned ears and lips and finished fleshing the hide, I took a hike up the mountain to retrieve the caribou skull we had encountered earlier. Later in the day, Bob used the satellite phone to make arrangements for the pilot to meet us at Butte Lake the following afternoon.

Early on the morning of August 3rd, we loaded up gear, tents and the sheep for the dreaded march to our pick-up point. With the addition of the horns and full cape (wet from its rinsing in the creek), I know I was carrying more weight than I had ever hauled before—about 90 pounds. The trek was an ordeal for all of us. In addition to the weight we carried and the tough going, we were deprived of water for the second half of the trip, as there were no suitable places to fill our water bottles. Despite the difficulty we arrived at our rendezvous point in less than six hours. To be honest, I came close to quitting around the five-hour mark, but I was proud that I had toughed it out!

Less than an hour after we arrived at the beach, the float plane could be heard as it descended for its impending landing on the lake. Karla was to be transported to the outfit's main camp, so we said our goodbyes. With plenty of hunting days remaining, Bob and I had the option of pursuing other animals, such as moose and caribou. However, I was so content—so complete—that taking the life of another animal would have seemed more like killing and less like hunting. I had everything I had come to the Yukon for; I wanted nothing more! Consequently, upon the pilot's return, Bob and I headed back to Whitehorse.

Most of Bob's family lives in Whitehorse and, much to my surprise, Bob arranged for me to stay with him at his parents' house. This was especially generous and, in my view, vastly superior to spending the remainder of my time in the Yukon in one of the city's downtown hotels. Delicious pizza, a shave and shower, and a night's sleep in a real bed capped the remainder of a very long and arduous day. I was able to rearrange my flights and leave for home the following afternoon. Unfortunately, because all the necessary paperwork wasn't complete, my sheep didn't depart Canada with me. Three long months would pass before I was reunited with my trophy!

The hunt had been short in its duration and spectacular in its outcome. Given my last two adventures, I didn't feel the slightest twinge of guilt about either. I guess things have a way of evening out over the long run. I took a great ram, the best of my career. While that's reason enough for celebration, in and of itself, taking a fabulous trophy neither makes me a great hunter nor does it make the hunt special. What truly elevates the significance of this hunt has less to do with the quality of the animal whose life happened to intersect mine on that mountain in the Yukon, and more to do with the trials and tribulations that I had to endure in order to get to that meeting point.

In its own and unique way, each and every sheep hunt is about pushing your limits and persevering when times get tough. My experiences over the past four years are, perhaps, just an extreme example of the sheep-hunting ethos. Because of the obstacles placed in my way and the difficulty in overcoming them, this hunt—marking my resurrection as a sheep hunter—will always enjoy an exalted place in my heart! By the grace of God I was once again blessed with an opportunity to participate in the greatest challenge hunting has to offer, and to do so on my own terms—my ram on my back. In the process, I was able to complete my second Grand Slam® with an open-sighted muzzleloader and my third overall. While I'm certainly proud of my accomplishments, more than anything else, I consider myself a very fortunate man!

This photo was taken through the spotting scope. The big ram can be seen in the center of the shot, feeding in a patch of green vegetation.

Photo by Bob House

This shot was taken from our last surveillance post the day before the hunting season began. The rams are at the far end of the valley, low on the mountain. Our final stalk followed a line about half way up the slope on the left.

Guide Bob House keeps an eye on the rams from afar, as we wait for them to move someplace more favorable to completing our final stalk.

A beautiful ram by any measure. Lady Luck shined brightly this day!
Photo by Bob House

Author's Biography

Paul C. Carter has been an avid big-game hunter for more than forty years. Like many others, the first animal he hunted was the white-tailed deer. Paul is a dedicated deer-tracking enthusiast and he has written a book on that subject. In addition to his exploits in pursuit of North America's most hunted animal, Paul has hunted and taken numerous big-game animals from Mexico to Alaska, many with a muzzle-loading rifle. Besides whitetails, his other hunting passion is wild sheep, and the mountains they inhabit. He has three Grand Slams® of North American wild sheep to his credit, two of which were accomplished using a muzzleloader sporting open sights—the only occasions when this feat is believed to have been achieved by a hunter.

Paul is married to Janet, his wife of thirty-seven years. They have two grown sons and currently live in Dalton, Massachusetts, where they enjoy their country home and the wildlife that frequents the property—especially the deer.

Visit Paul on the web @ www.paulccarter.com

Other Books—*Tracking Whitetails: Answers to Your Questions; Great Shot!: A Guide to Acquiring Shooting Skills For Big-Game Hunters*

Printed in the USA
CPSIA information can be obtained
at www.ICGtesting.com
LVHW011036221023
761799LV00037B/685